MAME

Book by

JEROME LAWRENCE *and* ROBERT E. LEE

Based on the novel by Patrick Den

MAME

Music and Lyrics by

JERRY
HERMAN

the play "Auntie Mame" by Lawrence and Lee

RANDOM HOUSE · New York

FOREWORD

Although our love affair with Mame spans more than a decade, we approached her as the central figure of this musical as if we were meeting the lady for the first time.

To spark the musical *Mame* with a life of her own, we did our best to forget we had written the play *Auntie Mame*. And a very pleasant miracle happened. Usually the conversion of a straight play into a musical means bleeding off the believability when the trumpets start blowing, and the musical tends to be a cartoon of the play on which it was based. But the opposite seems to have happened here.

Many minds have shaped this remarkable lady: Patrick Dennis, who created her in his best-selling novel, and now Jerry Herman, who has written a score which underscores the truth and warmth of the people who populate Three Beekman Place.

Mame herself seems to have plunged into the joyful work of making this musical. She is an almost unique figure in modern fiction: Mame refuses to be imaginary! She is not a fondly Remembered Mama or a Matchmaker going back to the gaslights of Fourteenth Street. Mame is more interested in torches along the Ganges and the lightning-bugs of Peckerwood. She virtually pole-vaults out of the gaiety of the Twenties into lunar orbit, soaring high above depressions, wars and worries, taking with her a wide-eyed little boy.

We always long for what we don't have. This seems to be the Year of the Mole—a time of blindness and confusion, of fuzzy aims and fading faith. Our theater lately has been in a dark age, reflecting only shadows. Mame somehow lifts a flame in that blackness. She has optimism! zest! bounce! Even when she isn't quite sure where she's going, Mame knows, by God, she'll get there!

All of us, even the most despondent and disillusioned, would like to be like Mame. Or we wish she would take us by the hand, as she does Patrick, and convince us that our planet isn't such a shabby place. We want to hear her sing "Open a New Window" in a decade when so many of us are pulling down the blinds and locking the shutters in pretended security. Mame is fun, but not mere escapist fare: she sings out a wish to run *toward* life, not away from it.

We have seen Mame's indomitable spirit embodied in dozens of stars in dozens of countries. Her battles with Mr. Babcock and her romance with Beau have been eloquently expressed in the major languages of the earth. But no translation could be more fortunate than the musical language of Jerry Herman. And no one could lift the flame of Mame higher than Miss Angela Lansbury.

But the audience is always the thermometer of the theater. A blazing conception can sputter out like a match in an ice-cube tray unless it sends its singular incandescence across the footlights. The flame of Mame actually comes from everyone who is warmed by her daring and set aglow by her impudent but loving laughter.

Jerome Lawrence
Robert E. Lee

MAME *was first produced in New York City by Fryer, Carr and Harris at the Winter Garden Theatre on May 24, 1966, with the following cast:*

(IN ORDER OF APPEARANCE)

PATRICK DENNIS, AGE 10	Frankie Michaels
AGNES GOOCH	Jane Connell
VERA CHARLES	Beatrice Arthur
MAME DENNIS	Angela Lansbury
RALPH DEVINE	Ron Young
BISHOP	Jack Davison
M. LINDSAY WOOLSEY	George Coe
ITO	Sab Shimono
DOORMAN	Art Matthews
ELEVATOR BOY	Stan Page
MESSENGER	Bill Stanton
DWIGHT BABCOCK	Willard Waterman
ART MODEL	Jo Tract
DANCE TEACHER	Johanna Douglas
LEADING MAN	Jack Davison
STAGE MANAGER	Art Matthews
MADAME BRANISLOWSKI	Charlotte Jones
GREGOR	John Taliaferro
BEAUREGARD JACKSON PICKETT BURNSIDE	Charles Braswell
UNCLE JEFF	Clifford Fearl
COUSIN FAN	Ruth Ramsey
SALLY CATO	Margaret Hall
MOTHER BURNSIDE	Charlotte Jones
PATRICK DENNIS, AGE 19–29	Jerry Lanning
JUNIOR BABCOCK	Randy Kirby
MRS. UPSON	Johanna Douglas

Mr. Upson	John C. Becher
Gloria Upson	Diana Walker
Pegeen Ryan	Diane Coupe
Peter Dennis	Michael Maitland

Mame's Friends

Diana Baffa, Jack Blackton, David Chaney, Pat Cummings, Jack Davison, Hilda Harris, Tommy Karaty, Nicole Karol, Gene Kelton, Nancy Lynch, Art Matthews, Ross Miles, Stan Page, Ruth Ramsey, Betty Rosebrock, Scotty Salmon, Bella Shalom, Bill Stanton, John Taliaferro, Jo Tract, Jodi Williams, Kathy Wilson.

Settings Designed by William and Jean Eckart
Costumes Designed by Robert Mackintosh
Lighting by Tharon Musser
Musical Direction and Vocal Arrangements by
Donald Pippin
Orchestrations by Philip J. Lang
Dance Music Arranged by Roger Adams
Assistant Choreographer Tom Panko   *Hair Styles by*
Ronald De Mann
Associate Producer John Bowab
Dances and Musical Numbers Staged by Onna White
Directed by Gene Saks

SYNOPSIS OF SCENES

The action takes place in Mame's Beekman Place apartment and various locales in which she becomes involved during a period from 1928 to 1946.

ACT ONE

1. Somewhere in New York, 1928
2. Mame's apartment
3. Hallway of Mame's apartment
4. Mame's bedroom
5. Mame's living room (and all around New York)
6. Mame's apartment
7. Shubert Theatre—New Haven
8. *Salon Pour Messieurs*
9. Mame's apartment
10. Peckerwood

ACT TWO

1. Prep School and College (and Singapore)
2. Mame's apartment
3. Mame's apartment, six months later
4. Upson Farm
5. Mame's apartment
6. Mame's apartment, 1946

MUSICAL NUMBERS

ACT ONE

"St. Bridget"	AGNES and PATRICK
"It's Today"	MAME and ALL
"Open a New Window"	MAME and ALL
"The Man in the Moon"	VERA, MAME and ALL
"My Best Girl"	PATRICK and MAME
"We Need a Little Christmas"	MAME, PATRICK, AGNES, ITO and BEAU
"The Fox Hunt"	UNCLE JEFF, PATRICK, COUSIN FAN, MOTHER BURNSIDE and COUSINS
"Mame"	BEAU and ALL

ACT TWO

"Mame" (reprise)	PATRICK
"My Best Girl" (reprise)	PATRICK
"Bosom Buddies"	MAME and VERA
"Gooch's Song"	AGNES
"That's How Young I Feel"	MAME and ALL
"If He Walked Into My Life"	MAME
"It's Today" (reprise)	MAME and ALL
"My Best Girl" (reprise)	PATRICK
"Open a New Window" (reprise)	MAME

Act One

Scene: Somewhere in New York. There is a pattern of terrifying city lights: a girl's huge, gartered leg kicking, a bubbling champagne glass, a flashing red arrow which points God-knows-where.

PATRICK, *age ten, and* AGNES GOOCH, *a dowdy nanny, face upstage as the end of the overture blends into the cacophonous sound of traffic and confusion. Each carries a suitcase, and clutches the other's hand. Slowly they turn around in a spotlight, gaping at the mystery of the big city.*

PATRICK   Golly, New York is like a foreign country!

AGNES   You don't have to worry, Patrick. I'm worried enough for both of us. (*Reaching into her reticule*) Now, all we've got to do is what the lawyer told us. (*Panicky*) The letter! I've lost the letter!

PATRICK (*Taking a crumpled letter out of his pocket, reasonably*)   You gave it to me, Agnes—after you lost your reading glasses.

AGNES (*Eyes to heaven*)   Thank you, St. Bridget. Read it again, Patrick.

PATRICK (*Reading*)   "Dear Miss Gooch. Herewith are instructions from the will of the late Edwin Dennis." (AGNES *puts her arm around the boy protectively*) "Upon

3

my demise, I direct our faithful nanny, Agnes Gooch, to deliver my son Patrick to my sister and only other living relative, Mame Dennis, at Three Beekman Place, New York City. However, the Knickerbocker Bank is appointed trustee with sole authority . . ."

AGNES (*Interrupting*) We don't need that part now. All we need is a safe haven. Oh, I've read about what happens after dark in New York—to unmarried girls and innocent children! Your dear Auntie must be worried frantic.

(AGNES *clasps her hands in prayer and sings*)
St. Bridget deliver us to Beekman Place
Away from the wicked and depraved,
A gray head is peeping through the curtain lace
Calling, "Come ye inside where you'll be saved."
She's baked him a cherry pie and glazed a ham,
Her dear arms reach out for his embrace,
So if you have pity on this poor lost lamb,
God love you,
Dear St. Bridget deliver us to Beekman Place!

Sing with me, Patrick. It'll keep up your courage.

PATRICK My father was a Presbyterian, Agnes. I don't think he'd like it.

AGNES Where your father is now, there's not much he can do about it. Sing!

PATRICK and AGNES (*Singing together*)
So if you have pity
On these poor lost sheep,

4

AGNES
> God love you,

AGNES and PATRICK
> Dear St. Bridget deliver us to Bee-eeeee-eekman
> Place!
> *(The light fades on their faces. There is a slap of
> raucous Dixieland as they go off)*

Scene: MAME's *elegant apartment atop Beekman Place. A cocktail party of the Twenties is at its inebriated height.*

A spotlight hits the top of a free-standing staircase. MAME, *in gold pajamas, has a bugle to her lips, and she sounds a phrase of "It's Today." The orchestra blasts an answer.*

VERA   Mame, what the hell are we celebrating?

OTHERS   Yeah, what's the occasion, Mame? What *are* we celebrating?

MAME   A holiday. One I just invented. The moon's full! The gin's in the bathtub. And all my dearest friends are here—even the ones I haven't met yet! (*Singing*)
    Light the candles,
    Get the ice out,
    Roll the rug up,
    It's today!

    Though it may not be anyone's birthday,
    And though it's far from the first of the year,
    I know that this very minute
    Has history in it,
    We're here!

MAME

ALL

It's a time for
Making merry,
And so I'm for
Makin' hay,

MAME

Tune the grand up,
Dance your shoes off,
Strike the band up,

ALL

It's today!
(Now MAME *is down the stairs greeting and kissing* GUESTS *who include: the half-drunken but chic operetta star,* VERA CHARLES; *a bearded Orthodox* BISHOP; *the athletic* RALPH DEVINE; *the suave publisher,* M. LINDSAY WOOLSEY; *and* PEOPLE *who might be Floyd Gibbons, Marian Anderson, Radcliffe Hall, Paul Robeson, Lady Mendl, Fatty Arbuckle, Bob Benchley, Texas Guinan, Alexander Woollcott, plus assorted* FLAPPERS, GANGSTERS, *and even an* ARAB)

MAME and ALL

And we're livin'!
And we're well, gang,
So raise hell, gang,
While we may—

MAME

> Call the cops out,
> Raise a racket,
> Pull the stops out,

ALL

> Pull out the stops

MAME and ALL

> It's today!
>
> Light the candles,
> Fill the punch bowl,
> Throw confetti,
> It's today!

VERA and BOOP-BOOP-A-DOOP GIRLS

> Life can also be lived on a weekday,
> So don't depend on a holiday date,
> If you need New Year's to bubble,
> Then order a double
> And wait,

MAME and ALL

> There's a thank you
> You can give life,
> If you live life
> All the way,
> Pour the Scotch out,
> Hold the roof down,

MAME

> Fellas, watch out,

8

MAME and ALL
It's today!

(MAME *has been perched on the piano as it was propelled around the apartment. Now she gathers the whole party in a huddle for the latest joke, and they scream with laughter.* ITO *leads* PATRICK *and* AGNES *into the midst of the madness*)

AGNES   This isn't Number Three Beekman Place, is it?

ITO   Oh, yes. You wait here. Missy Dennis having *affair* now.

(AGNES *reacts with shock.* LINDSAY *takes* MAME's *arm*)

LINDSAY   Why don't you marry me, Mame?

MAME   And lose you as a friend?

(*The* GUESTS *Charleston and generally cut up in 1928 style*)

MAME and ALL (*Singing*)
It's a time for
Making merry,
And so I'm for
Makin' hay,
Tune the grand up,
Call the cops out,
Strike the band up,
Pull the stops out,
Hallelujah,
It's today!

(MAME, *at the top of the stairs, sounds the bugle again and slides down the banister.* PATRICK *aches to be a part of the party, but* AGNES *pulls him toward the door*)

AGNES   Patrick, if anybody here's your Auntie Mame, it's better you never know.

PATRICK (*Protesting*)   I don't want to go. She's the first lady bugle-player I ever saw.

MALE GUEST (*Leaving*)   'Night, Mame.

MAME   Goodnight, Frank. See you Tuesday at the Algonquin. (*A* FEMALE GUEST *wiggles her torso sexily toward the exit*) Watch it, Edna!

PATRICK (*Approaching* MAME)   Can you play reveille?

MAME (*Moving toward the bar*)   Reveille? It's not one of my favorites.

PATRICK   I learned it at day camp. But I never had my own bugle. My Dad said it was too noisy.

MAME (*Giving him a soft drink*)   I *love* noise. You must come from a dreadful family.

PATRICK   I've only got one relative in the world.

MAME   Who's that?

MAME

PATRICK *You.*

AGNES (*Moving closer*) That's right.

MAME (*Staring at* AGNES *quizzically*) Who are you?

AGNES Gooch. I'm your nanny-in-law.

MAME But that's impossible. You're not coming until to-morrow. Your telegram said very clearly December first. This is November thirty-first. And everybody knows "Thirty days hath September, April, June and . . ." Omigod, I'm your Auntie Mame! (*Reaching under the bar for the bugle, and handing it to* PATRICK) And this is for you. A present.

PATRICK (*Taking the bugle*) Golly.

MAME (*Crossing to the center of the room, quieting the* CROWD) Listen, everybody. This is *my little boy!*

VERA What?

CROWD Why, Mame! We never knew.

MAME Well, he's not actually *my* little boy. He's my brother's son. From Des Moines. My poor late brother. (*Some sympathetic clucks. One hiccup*) This little tyke. In all the whole wide world, I'm his only living relative. And he's my only living relative. That's all we have, just each other, my little love. What was your name again?

PATRICK   Patrick. Patrick Dennis.

MAME   Would you like a mart—? Is it your bedtime? Heavens, it can't be. Or food? Food, that's it. You must be famished. You run along over there and help yourself to the caviar . . . (*Some* GANGSTERS *help* PATRICK *to some caviar*) After that, you can go upstairs and read a book or something.

RALPH DEVINE (*Approaching* MAME)   Mame! You're not going to let that child *read!* Taste life second hand.
        (PATRICK *turns, munching a canapé*)

MAME   Shake hands with Ralph Devine. He runs a very advanced school down in the Village—the Laboratory of Life.

PATRICK (*Eagerly shaking hands with* RALPH)   Is it a military school? Do they wear uniforms?

RALPH (*Feeling* PATRICK's *biceps*)   In my school, young man, we don't wear *anything*.

MAME   It's heaven. (*Steering* PATRICK *around*) And this is Mr. M. Lindsay Woolsey. He publishes books.

PATRICK (*Pointing to the bearded* BISHOP)   Who's *he?*

MAME   A Lithuanian Bishop. Doesn't speak a word of English. Very stimulating man. (*The* BISHOP *bows.* MAME *turns* PATRICK *to face* VERA, *who is downing champagne*) And this is one of the great ladies of the

musical theater and your Auntie Mame's dearest friend,
Vera Charles. She just *loves* children.

VERA (*Distastefully*) Yes.
> (VERA *passes out. She is caught by* RALPH DEVINE
> *and two* GANGSTERS, *who lift her above their heads.*
> *She is stiff as a board, but the champagne glass is*
> *still to her lips*)

MAME (*Tipping up* PATRICK's *chin*) Have you noticed—
you're very handsome?

PATRICK   I guess it runs in the family. So are you.

MAME (*Suddenly, projecting her voice*) Listen, everybody! (*All turn to listen*) This *is* a holiday. It's Patrick's Day. (*A chord*) Not St. Patrick's Day. (*A chord*)
My Patrick's Day! (*Warmly, singing to* PATRICK)
> Light the sparklers,
> Crash the cymbals,

PATRICK
> Blow the bugle,
> It's today!

MAME
> Someone gave me a wonderful present,
> Something I needed—and yet never knew—
> So start the whistling and clapping,
> 'Cause under the wrapping
> Was you!

And we'll give life
Quite a tumble,
And we'll live life
All the way . . .
(MAME *leads* PATRICK *to an ottoman and perches herself on the arm of a couch which rides offstage.* MAME *waves jauntily as the party disperses in the opposite direction.* PATRICK *stares around him, delighted*)

ALL

Call the cops out,
Raise a racket,
Pull the stops out,
It's today!
(*The lights fade*)

SCENE 3

Scene: A hallway in MAME'S *apartment. It is two weeks later.*

The DOORMAN *wheels in a shiny new bicycle.* AGNES, *confused and frustrated, is holding boxing gloves in one hand and a cage of live white mice at arm's length in the other hand.*

DOORMAN   You want this in the boy's room, too?

AGNES   No. His room's full. And he's not gonna ride it up here. No, better leave it. Maybe *she* will.

>   (*The* ELEVATOR BOY *comes in, with a huge stuffed giraffe*)

ELEVATOR BOY   Should I put this thing in the guest room?

DOORMAN   You can't. The First Lady of the American Theater's in there—out cold!

ELEVATOR BOY   What the hell does she do—*live* here?

>   (*The* ELEVATOR BOY *goes off with the giraffe, and the* DOORMAN *with the bicycle. A* MESSENGER *carries in a huge globe of the world*)

MESSENGER   Sign here.

>   (AGNES *signs, juggling the white mice*)

AGNES I'm not sure I can stand it. I've been here two weeks and they've had thirteen cocktail parties.

MESSENGER Only thirteen?

AGNES She called one off. The bootlegger was sick that day. (*The* MESSENGER *goes off with the globe.* ITO, *in topcoat and upturned hat, comes on. He is carrying a package*) Thank God you're here. Take 'em quick.
(ITO *takes the cage of white mice from* AGNES)

ITO (*Pleased at the mice*) Boy's room very crowded. I put white mice in *your* room.

AGNES (*Calling after* ITO) Can't you put 'em in your room? *I've* got the rabbits!
(ITO *giggles and carries the cage off as* PATRICK *races on. He whirls a model airplane on a string and stick*)

PATRICK Where's Auntie Mame? I've got to show her something.

AGNES No, no! You can't go in there, Patrick. She said never to wake her up—this early in the afternoon.
(*But* PATRICK *races off. Blend to next scene*)

Scene: MAME's *bedroom. Subdued lights come up on a plush and feminine empress-sized bed.* MAME *slumbers blissfully on a mountain of pink pillows.* PATRICK *bursts in, swinging the model airplane in circles above her head.*

PATRICK   Auntie Mame! Look!

MAME (*Startled, opening her eyes*)   My God—bats!

PATRICK   It's the Spirit of St. Louis!

MAME (*Gesturing him away*) Please, darling, your Auntie Mame's hung. (*Quietly, hurt,* PATRICK *starts out of the bedroom*) Patrick. Come back. I'm terribly interested in all your projects. I just didn't expect Mr. Lindbergh to land on my bed before breakfast.

PATRICK (*Handing her the plane*)   Look!

MAME   Oh, that's charming. (PATRICK *pulls open the blinds and sunlight floods the bed.* MAME *covers her eyes*) Child, how can you *see* with all that light? (PATRICK *adjusts the blinds to a halfway open position*) That's better. Now, come give your Auntie Mame a good morning kiss. (PATRICK *rushes toward the bed*) Gently, gently. (PATRICK *kisses her on the cheek*) Oh, that was lovely. You'll make some lucky woman very happy some day.

17

PATRICK   Oh, I'm gonna be exactly like you and keep my relations with the opposing sex—(*Pulling a small notebook from his pocket, reading*)—*plutonic*. That's one of my new words.

MAME   *Platonic.* I'm glad to see you're keeping a list, the way Auntie Mame told you.

PATRICK   I got some zingers at your party yesterday. Some of 'em aren't even in the dictionary.

MAME   Read me the ones you don't understand.

PATRICK   (*Reading*)   Stinko. Karl Marx. Hotsy Totsy Club. Lesbian. Son-of-a- . . .

MAME   (*Tearing the page from the notebook*)   My, my, what an eager little mind. You won't need some of these words for months and months.
> (*She folds the page, puts it under the pillows.* ITO *enters*)

ITO   Mr. Babcock from Knickerbocker Bank telephone. Be here in five minutes.

MAME   Oh, God, I've been dodging him for days. Ito, go straighten up the living room so it looks respectable. (ITO *hurries out*) And Ito . . . (*But* ITO's *gone. She turns to* PATRICK) Patrick, tell Ito to hurry me up a light breakfast: black coffee and a sidecar. (PATRICK *dashes off.* MAME *climbs out of bed and struggles into a feathery*

negligee and mules as she shouts off) Vera! Get in here.
Vera! Where the hell are you? Vera!!!
　　　*(Two unsteady hands clutch at the wall. VERA, still
　　　in last night's crumpled party clothes, pulls herself
　　　in the room, attempting a pose of hauteur)*

VERA *(Foggily)*　Did somebody call me?
　　　(MAME drags a bundle of dresses from her closet)

MAME　Vera. I need you. *(Dumping the dresses on the
bed)* Patrick's trustee is on his way over here!

VERA　In the middle of the night? *(Blinking at the light)*
My God, that moon's bright!

MAME　Don't you realize, some horrible man is descend-
ing like a vulture to rob me of my child?

VERA *(Examining herself blearily)*　Somebody's been
sleeping in my dress!

MAME *(Rifling through the dresses)*　Oh, Vera.

VERA　Mame, what are you so excited about?

MAME　You can't know how I feel, Vera. You've never
been a mother.

VERA *(Loftily)*　I'll have you know that once in Pitts-
burgh I played Mother Cabrini. During Lent.
　　　(PATRICK enters with a tray)

PATRICK   Auntie Mame, Mr. Babcock's downstairs!

MAME   Not already!
      (VERA *takes the sidecar and downs it*)

MAME   Go make him feel right at home, just like Auntie
Mame taught you.

PATRICK (*Hurrying off*)   Sure, Auntie Mame.

VERA   Mame, you're being utterly hysterical.

MAME (*Gathering the dresses and going off*)   Vera, you
don't realize—this is *war!*

VERA   If you need any help, I'll be right here in No
Man's Land.
      (VERA, *fully dressed, climbs into* MAME's *bed, pull-
ing the covers up over her head as the lights fade*)

SCENE 5

Scene: *The living room of* MAME'*s apartment immediately following. The puritanical* MR. BABCOCK *is waiting impatiently.* PATRICK *bounds down the stairs.*

PATRICK Mr. Babcock?

BABCOCK That's right, Sonny.

PATRICK We've been expecting you. My name is Patrick Dennis.

BABCOCK (*Shaking* PATRICK'*s hand*) Well, you look like a bully little chap. Yes sir, a bully little chap.

PATRICK (*Politely*) You look very bully, too, Mr. Babcock.

BABCOCK (*Sitting*) Say, I have a boy just about your age up in Darien. We'll have you up soon, and Junior can show you his cigar-band collection.

PATRICK (*Without enthusiasm*) That'll be swell. (*There is an awkward pause. What do they say to each other?*) Would you care for a martini, Mr. Babcock?

BABCOCK (*Frowning*) I don't think this is exactly the time . . .

21

PATRICK (*Blithely, crossing to the bar*) Oh, it's all right. Mr. Woollcott says *somewhere* in the world the sun is always just below the yard-arm. (PATRICK *plops ice cubes into a pitcher, pours in a great quantity of gin, and stirs*) Stir, never shake. Bruises the gin.

(PATRICK *uncorks the vermouth, pours a smidgen into a glass, sloshes it around, then empties it completely. Deftly, he pours the iced gin into the glass, tears a twist of lemon peel into it, and serves* BAB- COCK. MAME *sweeps down the stairs, wearing a sedate dress and the convincingly grand air of a Scarsdale matron*)

MAME Why, Mr. Babcock. What an honor to have you in our little home. Though I wonder if it makes the best first impression on a sensitive young mind to see you drinking during business hours.

BABCOCK (*Floundering*) But he . . .

MAME Don't you worry, I won't breathe a word to the Knickerbocker Bank.

BABCOCK Where did that youngster learn to mix a martini?

MAME (*Composed, sitting*) Mr. Babcock. Knowledge is power.

BABCOCK (*Sitting*) That is exactly what I'm here for. To discuss this youngster's education. His *proper* education.

MAME (*Clearing her throat*) Well, I feel . . .

BABCOCK I have a list of better boys' schools in Manhattan.

MAME Personally, I prefer coeducational.

BABCOCK What do you mean?

PATRICK That means when boys and girls go to the same . . .

BABCOCK I know. I know. (*Taking out a long envelope*) First on my list is the Barkley School, which is known to be splendid.

MAME Have you considered a wonderfully progressive school down in the Village . . .

BABCOCK Your late brother was very explicit in his will: he said *conservative* schooling.

MAME But what Patrick needs is . . .

BABCOCK What this boy needs is stability. A school that is both exclusive and restricted.

MAME Exclusively *what* and restricted to *whom*?

BABCOCK Want to keep the riff-raff out of this lad's life.

MAME Now, look here, Mr. Babbitt.

BABCOCK   *Cock.* Babcock.
  (*He downs the martini in one gulp*)

MAME   Yes.

BABCOCK   Now, Miss Dennis, unless we can decide on
some proper school here in Manhattan, I'll insist he be
shipped up to *my* alma mater—St. Boniface in Massachusetts.

MAME   No, no, that's too far away. (*Rising, dismissing
him*) It was very good of you to drop by, Mr. Babcock.

BABCOCK   Have we settled everything?

MAME   We certainly have.

BABCOCK   (*Getting up*) Well. For a minute there I
thought we were going to have a little friction. (*Handing her a form*) Here's the application to Barkley
School. You take him down and enroll him at eight
A.M. tomorrow.

MAME   Don't worry, Mr. Babcock. Patrick and I know
exactly what to do with it.

BABCOCK   Bully!
  (BABCOCK *marches off.* MAME *slowly tears up the
  application blank*)

MAME   That bastard. (PATRICK *takes out his notebook
and pencil*) That word, dear, is bastard. (*Taking the*

notebook, moistening the pencil, and printing) B-A-S-
T-A-R-D. (*Grandly handing it back*) And it means Mr.
Babcock.

PATRICK (*Joyfully*) Y'mean, I don't have to go to that
Barkley School, Auntie Mame?

MAME You're going to see *life*, Patrick—not just the inside of a safe-deposit box.
  (*She takes* PATRICK'*s hand. She is seething with
  fury and determination*)

PATRICK Won't I have to go to school at all?

MAME (*Grabbing him by the shoulders*) Well, maybe
we'll enroll you in Ralph Devine's lovely Laboratory of
Life. Part time. But do you know who's going to be your
teacher most of the time, Patrick? *Moi!* (*The music
pings and begins faintly in the background*) I'm going
to show you things you never dreamed existed! Look—
out there!

PATRICK At what?

MAME At everything, my little love! (*Singing*)
  Open a new window,
  Open a new door,
  Travel a new highway
  That's never been tried before,
  Before you find you're a dull fellow
  Punching the same clock,
  Walking the same tightrope

25

As everyone on the block—
The fellow you ought to be is three dimensional,
Soaking up life
Down to your toes,
Whenever they say you're slightly unconventional,
Just put your thumb up to your nose,
And show 'em how to
Dance to a new rhythm,
Whistle a new song,
Toast with a new vintage,
The fizz doesn't fizz too long—
There's only one way to make the bubbles stay;
Simply travel a new highway,
Dance to a new rhythm,
Open a new window every day!

If you follow your Auntie Mame,
I'll make this vow, my little love:
That on the last day of your life,
You'll be smiling the same young smile
You're smiling now, my little love
If you wake up every morning,
And you pull aside the shutter,
And promise me
That these'll be
The first words that you utter:

(MAME *sings as she climbs the spiraling steps, with
the bright-eyed* PATRICK *in tow, the stairs turning
slowly. At the top, a window frame descends;*
MAME *and* PATRICK *sit, and it swings them out into
free space against a multicolored pattern of win-*

dows which appear on the drop behind them. PATRICK *joins excitedly in the song, as the window descends and the staircase slides off.*

A parade of fancifully costumed Manhattan characters parade onto the stage whistling "Open a New Window." There are POLICEMEN, NEWSBOYS, BALLERINAS, ORGAN GRINDERS, WAITRESSES, CAB DRIVERS—*a colorful potpourri of people, seen through* PATRICK's *bedazzled eyes.*

MAME *and* PATRICK *join with these citizens of the most fabulous city of the world, serpentining about, then skipping, then marching as they sing)*

MAME (*Singing*)
    Open a new window,
    Open a new door,
    Travel a new highway
    That's never been tried before,
    Before you find you're a dull fellow
    Punching the same clock,
    Walking the same tightrope,
    As everyone on the block—
    The fellow you ought to be is three dimensional,
    Soaking up life
    Down to your toes,

MAME and PATRICK
    Whenever they say you're slightly unconventional,

PATRICK
    Just put your thumb up to your nose,

MAME and PATRICK
> And show 'em how to

ALL
> Dance to a new rhythm,
> Whistle a new song,
> Toast with a new vintage,
> The fizz doesn't fizz too long—
> There's only one way to make the bubbles stay;
> Simply travel a new highway,
> Dance to a new rhythm,
> Open a new window every day!

> Open a new window,
> Open a new door,
> Travel a new highway
> That's never been tried before,
> Before you find you're a dull fellow
> Punching the same clock,
> Walking the same tightrope,
> As everyone on the block—
> The fellow you ought to be is three dimensional,
> Soaking up life
> Down to your toes,
> Whenever they say you're slightly unconventional,
> Just put your thumb up to your nose,
> And show 'em how to
> Dance to a new rhythm,
> Whistle a new song,
> Toast with a new vintage,
> The fizz doesn't fizz too long—
> There's only one way to make the bubbles stay;

Simply travel a new highway,
Dance to a new rhythm,
Whistle a new love song,
Toast with a new vintage,
Open a new window every day!

(*The lighting changes suddenly.* MR. BABCOCK *crosses through the dispersing* CROWD. *He carries a notebook and seems to be looking for someone. As he goes off, a scantily draped* MODEL *appears from the left on a pedestal. An* ARTIST *in a beret is busy sketching her. We cannot see the canvas, but* MAME *draws* PATRICK *into the* ARTIST'*s studio. The boy, reluctant to come face to face with a nearly nude model, covers his eyes, but* MAME *assures him that it's all right, takes him to the* ARTIST, *and introduces him. Cheerfully, the* ARTIST *shows* PATRICK *and* MAME *the canvas on which he has been working: it is pure cubism. Its wheels and gears bear no external resemblance to the feminine form on the pedestal.*

The lights fade quickly. At stage-right, a wild modern dance duo is rehearsing a flapping, birdlike piece of primitive choreography as a stern old DANCE TEACHER *watches, beating time with her gold-topped staff.* MAME *introduces* PATRICK *to the* DANCE TEACHER *and goes off—to make her next change.* PATRICK *watches, fascinated; then the stern* DANCE TEACHER *holds out her staff as if it were a barre;* PATRICK *grasps it, limbers up a bit, then joins in the crazy dance, finally hopping off to the right on one foot with the others.*

*In the sudden dark, a fire siren begins to wail.
Then there are beams of red light and a projection
of crackling flames against the backdrop. As* FIRE-
MEN *hasten across the stage,* BABCOCK *crosses again,
wandering among them, still looking for* PATRICK.
But again, BABCOCK *just misses seeing him. A long
ladder, drawn by one* FIREMAN *to symbolize the
hook and ladder truck he is driving, rushes across
the stage, from right to left. And who is riding on
the back of the truck?* PATRICK *and* MAME! *They
wear fireman's gear and wave jauntily.*

*Next, we are in a speakeasy. A "Happy New
Year" sign overhead suggests a ceiling. A husky*
BOUNCER *stands by the bolted door at the left. The
speakeasy* CROWD *is doing an exotic tango. All of
the* MEN *have gleaming, slicked-down hair, and re-
semble Rudolph Valentino. In the middle of the
tango, there is a knock at the door. Everything
holds. The* BOUNCER *opens the tiny peephole.* PAT-
RICK'*s face appears)*

PATRICK   *Mame* sent me!
(Instantly, PATRICK *is admitted, followed by* MAME
*in a silver lamé, monkey-fur-trimmed coat. Immedi-
ately, they join the dance as the music continues.
Ten-year-old* PATRICK, *in knee pants, is the only
male without the Valentino hairdo. But he and*
MAME *out-tango them all!*

*At the peak of the dance, a police whistle sounds.
It's a raid! The* DANCERS *scatter, trying to escape
through a door upstage which is soon blocked by*
POLICEMEN.

MAME *pretends to have lost an earring, giving everybody else in the speakeasy a chance to sneak out the window. A* POLICEMAN *gets down on his hands and knees, trying to help her find it. While they are so occupied,* PATRICK *gets her coat and they try to make a break for freedom—but the* COPS *are in hot pursuit.*

In the darkness, the ENSEMBLE *is singing "Open a New Window," in unison. Then we see them all cross from the left to the right. A* POLICEMAN *carrying a steering wheel is in the lead, apparently driving a paddy wagon. The arrested celebrators follow him, crouched as if handcuffed in the paddy wagon, singing straight front as they inch sideways across the stage. Two* POLICEMEN *bring up the rear, carrying a barred gate, which is obviously the rear door of the van)*

MAME and ALL
    Open a new window,
    Open a new door,
    Travel a new highway
    That's never been tried before,
    Before you find you're a dull fellow
    Punching the same clock,
    Walking the same tightrope,
    As everyone on the block—
    The fellow you ought to be is three dimensional,
    Soaking up life
    Down to your toes,
    Whenever they say you're slightly unconventional,
    Just put your thumb up to your nose,

And show 'em how to
Dance to a new rhythm,
Whistle a new song,
Toast with a new vintage,
The fizz doesn't fizz too long—
There's only one way to make the bubbles stay;
Simply travel a new highway,
Dance to a new rhythm,
Open a new window every day!

(*The last of the* ARRESTEES *are* MAME *and* PATRICK. *Are they embarrassed? Not in the least. It's a new experience, another aspect of* PATRICK's *total education! They hug as the lights fade*)

Scene: The Beekman Place apartment. The décor has been changed, and the room is filled with pictures and statues of mothers and madonnas.

BABCOCK *is pacing.* AGNES *is coming down the stairs carrying a brightly colored blanket.*

BABCOCK Where is she? Where is that madwoman? Where is that deceitful Bohemian Delilah?

AGNES If you mean Miss Dennis, she's out buying presents for the boy.

BABCOCK Spoiling him rotten. My God, he hasn't even been going to school.

AGNES Oh, yes he has—to the Laboratory of Life.

BABCOCK The Laboratory of Life! That's no school. It's the Garden of Eden! I dropped by Barkley to check on the kid's academic standing. And what did I find? He isn't even registered. Never has been. So I've been hunting in every low, half-baked school for the feeble-minded in this town. And finally I found him—in the lowest of them all. There they were, a whole schoolroom of 'em: boys, girls, teachers, romping around stark naked. (*Thundering at* AGNES) Would you put a child of yours in a place like that?

33

AGNES   I'm unmarried.
  (*She disappears into the kitchen with the blanket*)

MAME (*Entering*)   What a day, Lindsay. What a lovely, lovely day.

LINDSAY (*Following her with packages*)   What a day is right. I haven't even had a chance to call my office.

MAME   Why, Mr. Babcock—what a surprise!

BABCOCK   You're no more fit to raise a child than Jezebel.

MAME (*Alarmed*)   Patrick. Something's happened to my Little Love!

BABCOCK   Get in here, you little heathen.
  (AGNES *re-enters with* PATRICK, *who is draped in the brightly colored blanket*)

AGNES   He's been hiding in the kitchen.

MAME   Patrick, what's wrong?

PATRICK   We were just playing fish families.

BABCOCK   Fish families!

MAME   Show me, darling.

PATRICK   Well, Mrs. Devine and all the girls crouch down on the floor under the sun lamps—and they pretend to

34

be lady fishes, depositing their eggs in the sand. Then
Mr. Devine and all the boys do what gentlemen fish do.

MAME   What could be more wholesome or natural?

BABCOCK   Natural! It might be natural for a sardine.

MAME   (*At her full height*)   Mr. Babcock, I consider
your conduct most undignified.

BABCOCK   At least *I'm* wearing a vest. (*Starting toward
the door*) I'm getting out of this combination nudist
camp–opium den before you make me look like the
vice-president in charge of free love!

MAME   (*Clamping her hands over* PATRICK's *ears*)   Mr.
Babcock! Not in front of the B-O-Y!

BABCOCK   Tomorrow morning, I, me, personally—I'm taking this kid off to boarding school: St. Boniface Acad-
emy. And he's going to stay there.

MAME   I'll do whatever you say. If you'll only let the child
stay near me.

BABCOCK   He goes, and he goes tomorrow.

MAME   Mr. Babcock . . .

LINDSAY   Now, let's be reasonable about this . . .

35

BABCOCK   I'm going to turn this kid into a decent, God-fearing Christian if I have to break every bone in his body. You have him ready by eight o'clock sharp. And, kid, you'd better be wearing knickers!
(*To the tune of "Open a New Window" in a dictatorial tempo,* BABCOCK *marches off. The music, in a minor key, switches to a legato phrase*)

PATRICK   I want to stay with you, Auntie Mame.

MAME   St. Boniface probably isn't so bad. Agnes, take Patrick upstairs and get him ready for dinner. We'll talk about it later, darling.
(*Reluctantly,* PATRICK *goes up the stairs with* AGNES. MAME, *at the foot of the stairs, looks up helplessly.* LINDSAY *comes to her side, trying to comfort her*)

LINDSAY   Mame, I'm sorry. I'm really sorry.
(*The doorbell chimes insistently.* ITO *goes to answer*)

VERA (*Offstage, urgently*)   Mame, are you home? (VERA *bursts in*) Have you talked to your stockbroker? (*Seeing* MAME's *worried face*) Yes. I can see you have.

LINDSAY   What about her stockbroker?

VERA   Don't you know? He's called me half a dozen times, trying to locate both of you.

LINDSAY (*Paling*)   What happened?

VERA Oh, the Bears have done something terrible to the Bulls—or vice versa. (*The phone rings*) Anyhow, nothing's worth anything any more.

LINDSAY Don't you worry, Mame. I'm sure this is only something temporary.
  (ITO *has answered the phone, nodding pleasantly as he listens*)

ITO (*Cheerfully*) Missy Dennis. Stockbroker want to say hello before he jump out of window.
  (LINDSAY *grabs the phone*)

LINDSAY (*Into the phone*) How bad is it, Arthur? Everything? (*Stunned, he hangs up the phone*) Mame, I'm afraid you're wiped out. We all are.

VERA Thank God I never put anything aside.

MAME Who gives a damn about money? I've lost my child.

VERA What?

LINDSAY Patrick's trustee is sending him to school in Massachusetts.

VERA Oh, Mame darling, I know how you must feel.

LINDSAY (*Starting out*) I'll go right over to your stockbroker's and see if I can pick up the pieces.
  (*Helpless,* LINDSAY *goes off*)

MAME   Vera, what am I gonna do?

VERA   (*Putting her arm around* MAME, *nobly*)   Mame, I've got the perfect solution—the theater! (*She dramatically puts up a hand to stop* MAME's *protest*) I'll talk to J.J. and tell him he's simply *got* to give you a part in my new show. (*Gallantly*) And the Knickerbocker Bank is sure to let Patrick come back to you, when they find out you've settled down to something steady like acting.

MAME   Oh, you're so right, Vera. And if old Babcock still stands in the way, at least I'll be earning the money to *fight* him. It'll be like when we were in the chorus together.
       (*There is a deathly pause*)

VERA   *I* was never in the chorus.

MAME   About five hundred dollars a week to start, don't you think? And then there'll be a raise.

VERA   Mame, it'll only be a bit—at the end of the last act.

MAME   Oh, I accept, I accept. This isn't just charity? You really want me? Because of my talent.

VERA   (*What has she done?*)   I want you. I want you.

MAME   I just can't wait to hear that overture. (*The lights narrow on their faces, and there is the effect of an orchestra tuning up*) Tell me all about it, Vera.

MAME

VERA   Well, it's this terribly modern operetta about a lady
astronomer.

MAME   I've always wanted to be a lady astronomer.

VERA   *I'm* the lady astronomer. You're offstage right, waiting for your very exciting entrance at the most climactic
moment of the show. (*Eagerly,* MAME *goes off in the
direction* VERA *has indicated*) I teach in this girl's
seminary and I'm in love with a professor in this men's
seminary, but he's a terrible failure. Well, on the night
of the rising of the moon, I, a mere woman, make a
universe-shaking discovery. (*A baby-blue operetta show
curtain and a bulb-lined proscenium have descended behind* VERA. *Four* GIRL STUDENTS *in baby-blue caps and
gowns swirl around* VERA, *dressing her for her role.* VERA
*is handed a jewel-studded telescope. She is now com-
pletely costumed as a noble heroine, sprinkled with glittering rhinestone stars. Now we seem to be seeing the
actual performance, as* VERA *sings*)

   I have a little secret I'd like to impart
   That I hope doesn't give you too much of a start,
   Though it's shocking, it's completely true.
   I know it isn't gossip or rumor, of course,
   For I have it from quite a reliable source,
   And I'd like to pass it on to you . . .

   The man in the moon is a lady,
   A lady in lipstick and curls,
   The cow that jumped ovah
   Cried, "Jumpin' Jehovah,

39

I think it's just one of the girls!"
She winks at the stars
From her bed of green cheese;
That isn't a nightgown,
It's a Saturn chemise . . .
Oh, her friends are the stars and the planets,
She sends the Big Dipper a kiss,
So don't ever offend 'er,
Remember her gender,
The man in the moon is a miss.

    (*As* VERA *turns upstage, the show curtain rises.*)

Frankie Michaels and Angela Lansbury as PATRICK
and MAME.

Scene: The full stage of the Shubert Theatre in New Haven. There is a second bulb-lined proscenium, a cut-out of a mountain peak, and a sky-drop filled with twinkling stars.

In a swirl of music, more GIRL STUDENTS *come on, in blue caps and gowns, but only thigh length. They all dance on point.*

BOY STUDENTS, *also in baby-blue tights and waistcoats, swirl on from the other side. All carry telescopes. There is a sting and tremulo of music as the two groups meet at the foot of the mountain. The* LEADING MAN, *a typical baritone, is posed nobly on the mountainside.*

VERA (*Sweeping toward her* LEADING MAN) The stars have brought us together, my beloved. And now we shall have proof of my great discovery. For it is the time of the rising of the moon. (*All point to the sky and focus their twinkly telescopes toward it. The music trembles suspensefully, but nothing happens.* VERA *waits, points again, raising her voice*) The time of the RISING OF THE MOON! (*The orchestra and chorus repeat the anticipatory figure, but again nothing happens.* VERA *is suffering, but she manages a hollow laugh*) The RISING OF THE MOON is a bit late, my beloved. But we shall see it soon—in all its glory. (*She floats toward the wings and calls offstage*) Tell her to get her ass on that moon!

(MAME, *costumed in a flowing yellow moon-gown and wide-brimmed hat, sneaks on upstage. Now the moon rises, a crescent, with* MAME *draped in it.* MAME *sings a delicate and tinkling obligato, like the "Laugh Song," as* VERA *struggles through a repeat of the melody. But as* MAME *stares down, her fear carries her away and her obligato goes wild.* MAME *hangs onto the swaying moon for dear life, but her hat falls off and she ends up clinging to the underside of the crescent.* VERA, *in a rage, beats her telescope against the moon. She pushes through the confused dancers and beats time with her telescope, attempting to rush to the end of the song. She indicates a cut-off. When the speeded-up music doesn't cut off, she throws her telescope at the* CON-DUCTOR. *When the music finally finishes,* VERA *clutches her breast and storms offstage. By lighting effect, the curtain seems to fall. The moon is lowered jerkily, and* MAME *rushes forward to try to explain*)

STAGE MANAGER   Places for curtain calls! Miss Charles, Miss Charles. Places for curtain calls!

VERA (*Coming back onstage*)   This is the most disgraceful thing that has happened in the history of the theater!

MAME (*Crushed*)   Listen, everybody. This is my dearest friend. I owe my career to her, my whole comeback. (MAME *embraces* VERA. *But her bracelets clang together and she gets locked around* VERA's *middle*)

STAGE MANAGER   C'mon. Curtain calls.

VERA   Get offstage. Let go!

MAME   I can't. I'm *stuck*.
    (*The curtain rises for calls, and* VERA *tries to make
    a bow,* MAME, *still clutched around her midriff,
    half-sinks on her knees. As the curtain falls,* VERA
    shouts furiously)

VERA   Somebody get a pair of pliers. Get me loose! (*The*
    STAGE MANAGER *rushes onstage with pliers. But the cur-
    tain rises again. The* STAGE MANAGER, *caught onstage,
    also takes a bow*) That's enough.

STAGE MANAGER   That's enough. Strike the set. Work-
    light!
    (*The curtain has fallen for the last time. Scenery
    flies—so that only a work-light and a small stoop are
    left onstage. The backsides of set pieces read "The
    Lady Astronomer—Finale."* VERA *breaks loose from*
    MAME *and flings her angrily away*)

VERA   I've got a real astronomical discovery for you: the
    man in the moon is a BITCH!
    (VERA *storms off.* MAME, *alone onstage, watches the
    crescent moon disappear into the flies*)

STAGE MANAGER (*Calling*)   Nine o'clock call tomorrow
    morning. Replacement for the Moon Lady. (*Seeing*
    MAME) Sorry, Moon Lady.
    (*Now* MAME *is completely alone. She sinks to the*

43

stoop, in utter desolation. PATRICK *comes onstage, in an overcoat, and carrying a cap. He hesitates at the edge of the circle of light narrowed on* MAME)

PATRICK   I thought you were very good, Auntie Mame. Everybody noticed you.

MAME   My little love. How did you get to New Haven?

PATRICK   Ito brought me.

MAME   But how could he bring you, when I've already sold the car?

PATRICK   Oh, we didn't drive; we hitchhiked.

MAME   But Mr. Babcock thinks you're in that horrible school.

PATRICK   (*Sitting beside her*)   I told 'em it was sort of a lecture on astronomy, so they let me come.

MAME   Are you ashamed of your Auntie Mame?

PATRICK   I'm *proud* of you. Nobody liked the stinky old show until you came in.
(*The music begins, softly and tenderly*)

MAME   Oh, Patrick, I'm a failure.

PATRICK   No, you're not. Not to me. Not ever. (*Singing*)

You're my best girl,
And nothing you do is wrong,
I'm proud you belong to me;
And if a day is rough for me,
Having you there's enough for me.
But if some day
Another girl comes along,
It won't take her long to see
That I'll still be found
Just hangin' around
My best girl.

MAME (*Singing*)
You're my best beau,
You're handsome and brave and strong,
There's nothing we two can't face;
If you're with me, whatever comes,
We'll see that trouble never comes.
And if some day
Another beau comes along
Determined to take your place,
I hope he's resigned
To fall in behind
My best beau.

MAME and PATRICK (*Rising*)
And if some day
When everything turns out wrong,
You're through with the human race,
Come running to me,
For I'll always be

45

MAME
Your best girl.

PATRICK (*Offering his arm*)
My best girl.
(MAME *takes his strong young arm, and they go off together. The music rises and the lights fade*)

Scene: Salon Pour Messieurs. MADAME BRANISLOW-SKI, *a chic White-Russian martinet, supervises a men's beauty parlor.*

As the set comes in, BEAU *enters from the left. He is handsome and imposing in a camel's-hair coat. He pulls off his gloves.* MADAME BRANISLOWSKI *hurries on from the right in a distinctively flowered dress.*

MADAME   Welcome—welcome to my *Salon Pour Messieurs.*

BEAU   Pardon me, I think I'm in the wrong place.

MADAME   But you are the four o'clock appointment—Mr. Burnside.

BEAU (*Looking about, uncomfortably*)   That's right. But this seems more like a beauty salon *pour mesdames.*

MADAME   Why should the male not also be beautiful? (*Calling*) Gregor!
(*The curtains open and* GREGOR *flits in. His jacket is in the same flowered pattern. He takes* BEAU's *coat. A barber chair slides into place*)

BEAU   Thank you kindly.
(*He steps into the chair*)

47

MADAME   Naturally, we are giving you the full treatment. Facial, pedicure, mudpack.

BEAU   Mudpack? (*He laughs*) *I'll* just have a shave and a neck-trim. Oh, maybe a manicure.
(*He leans back in the chair.* GREGOR *tips it back and wraps a towel over* BEAU's *face.* MADAME *draws* GREGOR *aside*)

MADAME   Manicure? Gregor, who is available?

GREGOR   Only the new girl.

MADAME   Can we trust her? (GREGOR *shrugs.* MADAME *calls*) Miss Dennis!
(MAME, *in a smock of the same flowered pattern, and carrying a manicurist's tray, enters with an eager, open-faced, willing-to-be-of-service look*)

MAME   Yes, Madame. Here, Madame. Ready, Madame.

MADAME   (*Whispering to* MAME) Southern aristocracy. But with money. (*To* BEAU) I am giving you Miss Dennis. Our most experienced manicurist.

BEAU   (*From beneath the towel*)   Thank you.

MADAME   (*To* MAME)   Take very good care of him.

MAME   Oh, I will. I will. (MADAME *goes out*) Excuse me, Sir. Are you right-handed?

BEAU Yes.

MAME Maybe we'd better start with the left.
(MAME *pulls up a stool, and searches for* BEAU's
left hand. She starts to file)

BEAU (*Suddenly*) I wish to see the young lady who is
doing my nails.
(GREGOR *quickly unswirls the towel from his face,
switches the chair to an upright position, and goes
off.* MAME *and* BEAU *are face-to-face for the first
time, and holding hands.* MAME *stares at him, for he
is handsome, amiable, a hell of a guy*)

MAME (*Flustered*) Am I doing something wrong?

BEAU No, Ma'am! You have a very delicate touch, Miss
Dennis—is that your name?

MAME (*Staring at him*) Yes, Mr. . . .

BEAU Beauregard Jackson Pickett Burnside.

MAME (*Still holding his hand*) I'm certainly glad to
know you. I'd shake your hand, but I'm already shaking.
(*They laugh.* MAME *starts to file away at his nails.* BEAU
winces slightly) Oh. Did I get too close to the quick?

BEAU No, Ma'am. Down South, we all lean to short
nails.

49

MAME (*Dreamily*) The South. All that lovely, lost elegance.

BEAU Not completely lost, Ma'am. You'd just *love* Peckerwood.

MAME Peckerwood? Who's Peckerwood?

BEAU Why, that's the name of my plantation.
(*He winces*)

MAME I hurt you again!

BEAU Did you, Ma'am? I honest-to-gosh didn't notice.

MAME (*Dipping his left hand into the water and moving her stool to his right side*) You're so friendly and nice, I've just got to tell you the truth. (*Lowering her voice*) Madame told a big fib. I'm not her "most experienced manicurist." I just started. You're my first customer.

BEAU I'm honored, Ma'am. My hands are takin' a maiden voyage.

MAME What a lovely thing to say.
(*She keeps on filing, but stares into his face*)

BEAU It comes more or less natural sayin' lovely things to a lovely lady.

MAME What would your wife do if she heard you say that?

BEAU Raise tarnation, most likely. If I *had* a wife. Which I don't. (MAME *files faster*) But I've got practically every other kind of relative that's been invented.

MAME Are they all as nice as you?

BEAU You just oughta come down Georgia-way and meet us all one day.

MAME Why, I'd love to meet you all.
(MADAME *enters*)

MADAME How are we enjoying our manicure, Sir?

BEAU It's an extraordinary experience.

MADAME (*Staring at his hands, horrified*) This customer is *bleeding!*

BEAU Nothing, really—just a tiny little old scratch . . .

MADAME Nothing! (MADAME *clutches* BEAU's *hand, pulling him out of the barber chair*) I've never seen anything so horrible! Gregor, look! Look! (GREGOR *rushes on.* MADAME *brandishes* BEAU's *hand almost as if it were disconnected from his body*) The fingertip is almost gone!

MAME (*To* BEAU) I'm terribly sorry! I didn't mean to hurt you.

MADAME (*Imperiously, to* MAME) Out, out! Turn in your smock!

BEAU (*As he is dragged off*) It's honestly my fault. I distracted her. This little lady was doing an absolutely bang-up job.
  (MAME *takes off her smock, and reaches offstage for her coat and floppy hat*)

MAME You're a wonderful person. And brave. (*Defiantly, putting on her coat*) And you oughta get your manicures where they don't hire people like me.
  (*A total failure,* MAME *crosses disconsolately back toward her apartment*)

Scene: The Beekman Place apartment. To a wistful and minor "It's Today," MAME *enters her apartment—now denuded of its extravagant furnishings.*

MAME *(Calling, without spirit)* Agnes? Ito?
    *(*PATRICK *hurries down the stairs)*

PATRICK   Hi, Auntie Mame!

MAME *(Hugging him)* Darling! What are you doing home?

PATRICK   They gave me a long week-end, on account of good grades. I belong to you legally for three whole days.

MAME   Oh? I was hoping maybe you'd been expelled.
    *(*ITO *and* AGNES *emerge from the kitchen)*

ITO *(Brightly)* Missy get fired again?

MAME   I'm afraid so, Ito. I was just as bad at fingernails as I was at selling vacuum cleaners.

AGNES   I'm glad you're home, Miss Dennis. I didn't know what to fix for dinner.

MAME   What did we have last night?

53

AGNES   Shredded Wheat.

MAME   Agnes—Ito—I did hope I could pay you some of your back salary . . .

AGNES   I'm not money-mad, Miss Dennis; I wouldn't think of leaving you.

ITO (*Cheerfully*)   No place else get job anyhow.
    (*There is a strained moment.* MAME *looks from one face to the next, then at the blank walls, previously hung with expensive paintings—and she breaks: the pillar of the household collapses into tears*)

PATRICK   Please don't cry, Auntie Mame!

MAME   Hell, we don't even have any Kleenex!
    (AGNES *offers* MAME *a handkerchief from her sweater sleeve*)

AGNES   You're a loving woman, Miss Dennis. You're peculiar, but you're loving!
    (MAME *returns the handkerchief, patting* AGNES' *hand*)

MAME (*Through her tears*)   Thanks, Agnes. You're peculiar, too. (*She gets up with sudden resolve*) What are we doing, sitting around, letting the depression depress us? (*She pulls three packages from beneath the couch*) Merry Christmas, everybody!
    (*They are all astonished at this*)

ITO Missy Dennis get mixed up with calendar again. Not Christmas yet.

AGNES It says in the paper sixteen shopping days until.

MAME Well, we *need* it now, so let's go ahead and have it. (*Handing out the presents*) About three jobs ago, I bought these Christmas presents fast, before I was tempted to spend the money on something foolish like food.

PATRICK (*Eagerly tearing open a suit box*) Golly! Long pants! At last!
     (ITO *takes a wristwatch out of his package*)

ITO Oh, thank you, Missy.

MAME It's not Tiffany's, Ito. It's Walgreen's.

AGNES (*Unwrapping a bottle*) Perfume! It's so French-smelling.

MAME (*Suddenly*) What'd we do with last year's Christmas decorations?

ITO In kitchen closet.

MAME Go and get 'em! (ITO *runs off.* MAME *sings*)
     Haul out the holly,
     Put up the tree before my spirit falls again!
     Fill up the stocking,
     We may be rushing things, but deck the halls again
          now!
     For we need a little Christmas

Right this very minute,
Candles in the window,
Carols at the spinet,
Yes, we need a little Christmas
Right this very minute,
It hasn't snowed a single flurry,
But Santa dear, we're in a hurry—
So climb down the chimney,
Turn on the brightest string of lights I've ever seen,
Slice up the fruitcake,
It's time we hung some tinsel on that evergreen bough;
For I've grown a little leaner,
Grown a little colder,
Grown a little sadder,
Grown a little older,
And I need a little angel
Sitting on my shoulder,
Need a little Christmas now!

> (ITO *comes in with a box full of Christmas decorations. Intoxicated by* MAME's *enthusiasm, they deck one another with the trimmings of previous Christmases.* AGNES *even pins Christmas tree balls on as earrings*)

MAME and ALL
    Haul out the holly,

MAME
    Haven't I taught you well to live each living day?

MAME and ALL
    Fill up the stocking!

PATRICK

But Auntie Mame, it's one week past Thanksgiving
day now—

MAME, AGNES and ITO

But we need a little Christmas
Right this very minute,
Candles in the window,

ALL

Carols at the spinet,
Yes, we need a little Christmas
Right this very minute,

AGNES

It hasn't snowed a single flurry,
But Santa dear, we're in a hurry—

ITO

So climb down the chimney,
It's been a long while since I've felt good neighbor-ry,

ALL

Slice up the fruitcake,
It's time we hung some tinsel on that bayberry bough;
For we need a little music,
Need a little laughter,
Need a little singing
Ringing through the rafter,
And we need a little snappy
"Happy everafter,"
Need a little Christmas now!

57

(The dance is a parade, climaxing in an explosive polka)

PATRICK   Can I try on my long pants now, Auntie Mame? Right now?

MAME   *Right now.*
(PATRICK *bounds off*)

AGNES   But we don't have any presents for you.

MAME   Oh, Agnes.
(AGNES *whispers to* ITO, *who scampers into the kitchen*)

AGNES   Yes, we do. I hope you won't be angry about what we've done.
(ITO *rushes back in with a spindle of bills*)

ITO   Merry Christmas, Missy! (*Reluctantly,* MAME *takes the spindle of bills*) We pay bills—now butcher no give nasty look with lamb chops.

AGNES   Ito had some money put by, and so did I—for a rainy day. But it can't get much wetter than it is right now.

MAME   (*Touched*)   You're both so dear to me. I'll try to pay you back—someday.
(PATRICK *enters in his long pants*)

PATRICK Look!

MAME Wow!

PATRICK Hold out your wrist. (*Slipping a rhinestone bracelet on her outstretched arm*) With Christmas coming so quick, I didn't have time to wrap it.

MAME (*Marveling at the bracelet*) Where did you get the money?

PATRICK Well, I sort of made a trade at the pawnshop. I haven't been playing my bugle much, anyhow. I got a smooth one—so you won't get hooked again! (*Kissing her cheek, gently*) Merry Christmas, Auntie Mame.

ITO and AGNES Merry Christmas!

MAME and ALL (*Singing*)
  For we need a little music,
  Need a little laughter,
  Need a little singing
  Ringing through the rafter,
  And we need a little snappy
  "Happy everafter,"
  Need a little Christmas now!
    (*The doorbell chimes*)

MAME (*Bedecked with Christmas decorations and a Santa Claus beard*) If that's Santa Claus, tell him we've already had it!

(PATRICK *plops a Santa Claus cap on her head and she slips the beard onto her chin.* ITO *goes to the door and ushers in the apologetic* BEAU)

BEAU Miss Dennis, I'm delighted to see you again!

MAME (*Quickly pulling off the Santa Claus beard and cap*) After I sawed you up!

BEAU Little lady, I'm the one to apologize. I'm afraid you lost your position on my account.

MAME Oh, no, I'm very good at getting fired—all by myself.

BEAU The instant you took my hand, I sensed that you were not the kind of person who—what shall I say?—takes people's hands—uh—*commercially.*

MAME (*Sympathetically*) Oh, how is your hand?

BEAU (*Revealing bandaged fingers*) Healing like a house afire. I'll be able to get a glove on in a day or two.

MAME (*Flustered*) My goodness. Family, I want you to meet—Mr. Beauregard Jackson Pickett Burnside.

BEAU Remarkable memory, Miss Dennis. I sometimes forget part of it myself.
    (*They laugh*)

MAME   We've been having Christmas. It's a little early, but we're free-thinkers.

BEAU   I *like* that. I feel like Christmas, too. And I want to take all of you-all to dinner to celebrate. You go get your coats while I tell that cab to wait.
   (BEAU *goes out*)

PATRICK   He's nice.

AGNES (*Emphatically*)   Marry him. The minute he asks you.
   (*They rush for their coats*)

ITO (*Re-entering*)   Me never believe in Santa Claus. Me beginning to change mind.

MAME (*Dazed, as she is helped into her coat*)   Well, I never expected Santa Claus to look so much like Rhett Butler.
   (BEAU *reappears. The whole family is lined up waiting for him.* BEAU *takes* MAME's *arm. The other three link arms, and they start off*)

ALL (*Singing*)
   For we've *got* a little Christmas
   Right this very minute,
   Got a little Christmas now!
      (*Now they are on the streets of Manhattan*)
   For we've got a little Christmas
   Right this very minute,
   Candles in the window,

Carols at the spinet,
Yes, we've got a little Christmas
Right this very minute,
Got a little Christmas now!
   (*The lights fade*)

Scene: The portico and front lawn of Peckerwood. There is bluegrass and there are bluebloods: it is a gathering of the family, all in their Sunday best, to meet BEAU's *Yankee girl friend. The tone is roughly the same as that when General Sherman was received in Atlanta. Prominent in the gathering are the fluttering* COUSIN FAN *and the emaciated* UNCLE JEFF. *The background music is languid as molasses.*

JEFF Must be something mighty special about this Dennis woman if'n Beau skittles her all the way down here from New York City. Mornin', Cousin Fan.

FAN Peculiar mornin', Uncle Jeff. *Mighty* peculiar. Is it generally known that Beau and his lady friend have a *child* with them?
    (*Reactions of shock*)

JEFF No-o-o-o!

FAN And she hain't even *met* Mother Burnside yet.

JEFF Ho-ho. Looks like we're gonna have some fireworks here at Peckerwood.
    (SALLY CATO *sweeps on. She is a handsome, horsey woman*)

SALLY CATO Well, naow!

63

JEFF   Why, Sally Cato.

SALLY CATO   Hello, Jeff honey.

FAN   Didn't rightly 'spect *you* to be comin' round for the doin's.

SALLY CATO   (*Dripping sweetness*) How ever could I manage to stay away when me and Beau've been engaged since grammar school? I wouldn't feel like a true daughter of the South if I didn't ooze out all the hospitality that's just simmerin' in my innards!
   (*The* GUESTS *almost snap to attention as* MOTHER BURNSIDE *appears from within the house, on* BEAU's *arm. She is a massive octogenarian*)

MOTHER BURNSIDE   What do you mean I don't look happy, Beauregard? I'm always happy. (*She scrutinizes each* GUEST *disdainfully*) When are you gonna trot out that New York filly? All I can see around here is *family*.

BEAU   Now, Mother . . .

MOTHER BURNSIDE   'Ceptin' you, Sally Cato. (*To* BEAU) When we got peaches right here, ripe for the pickin', I cain't see why any man would go hankerin' after some *Northern* alligator pear.

BEAU   Mother, the War between the States is over.

MOTHER BURNSIDE   (*Dismissing such nonsense*) Don't give me any of that Appomattox applesauce.

64

SALLY CATO (*Kissing* BEAU's *cheek*) Welcome home, Beau sugah.

BEAU (*Uncomfortably*) Hello there, Sally Cato. (*Calling*) Mame! Mame honey, we're all out here, waitin' for you.

MAME'S VOICE (*Offstage, Southern as a candied yam*) Ah'm comin', Beau sugah. Ah'm just bustin' to meet yoah sweet little ol' mothah!
(MAME *sweeps on in a hoop skirt, looking like Scarlett O'Hara*)

BEAU Mother, may I present Miss Mame Dennis.
(*He steps aside, revealing the massive* MOTHER BURNSIDE)

MAME Oh, Miz Burnside, you're more than I expected.

BEAU And these are my kinfolk.
(MAME *stares around at the frozen faces*)

MAME Chowmed.

BEAU Oh, you'll all be first-namin' each other soon as I slosh another gallon of bourbon in the punch bowl.
(*He goes into the house with* MOTHER BURNSIDE. MAME, *alone, stares around uncomfortably.* SALLY CATO *slithers up to* MAME *with chummy unction*)

SALLY CATO I'm Sally Cato MacDougal. I could tell from

the first instant I set eyes on you that we was gonna be the closest of friends, Mame.

MAME Why, that's awfully kind of you, Sally Cato.

SALLY CATO Was it *horses* brought you and Beauregard together?

MAME Horses?

SALLY CATO My Beau would be bored blue with anybody who wasn't practically *born* on a horse.

MAME Well, I wasn't really *born* on a horse. (*Quickly*) But riding is my life. Dear me, every day, up at the crack of noon.

SALLY CATO That settles it. Here I've been wrackin' my poor brain tryin' to figure what *special* I could do to let you know how I feel about your bein' down here. And what could be sweeter than a *hunt!*

MAME (*Paling*) A hunt?

SALLY CATO Dawn tomorrow morning. And everybody's invited. (*There are exclamations of delight and approval*) Won't we have the lark, all of us—leapin' those hedges, jumpin' those river gaps, the hounds yappin' around those boulders. I tell you, Mame, every eye in this county is gonna be on *you* tomorrow mornin'!

MAME   If I'd only known. You see, I didn't bring along any of my riding togs.

SALLY CATO   Don't you worry, Mame child. I've got dozens of things you can wear. You do ride astride?

MAME   (*Grasping at straws*)   No, no. Sidesaddle. Always.

SALLY CATO   (*Purring*)   Now, isn't that grand? I have a little old sidesaddle that'll do you just *fine*.
     (BEAU *re-enters, with a tray of punch glasses;* PATRICK *is behind him*)

BEAU   Punch, ladies?
     (MAME *takes a cup of punch and keeps drinking it*)

SALLY CATO   Beau darlin', we're havin' a hunt. At dawn tomorrow. And you want to hear something fantastic? Your sweet little Yankee friend is gonna ride sidesaddle.

BEAU   I won't allow it. It's too dangerous.

SALLY CATO   But, darlin', she's insisted.

BEAU   Well, anything Mame says she can do, she can do.
     (*Quickly,* MAME *slams down her punch cup and picks up another*)

SALLY CATO   Mame sugah, I'm just gonna hold my breath until dawn tomorrow.

MAME   Do that, honey.
>   (*The lights fade. A grumpy rooster crows, indicating dawn. On the front lawn* HUNTSMEN *and* GROOMS *are gathering along with* MOTHER BURNSIDE, COUSIN FAN, JEFF *and* PATRICK. JEFF *confronts* MOTHER BURNSIDE)

JEFF   Mawnin', Mother Burnside. Did we get Miss Dennis a nice piece of horseflesh?

MOTHER BURNSIDE   We sure did. Lightnin' Rod.
>   (*From offstage, there is a fierce whinny and the stomping of angry hooves.* GROOMS *back away from it in terror*)

JEFF   Lightnin' Rod! Thought he went mad.

MOTHER BURNSIDE   Did.

PATRICK   My Auntie Mame is riding a mad horse?

MOTHER BURNSIDE   Temporarily.
>   (*Another angry whinny from Lightnin' Rod offstage*)

FAN   Nobody ever rode Lightnin' Rod and lived to tell about it.

MOTHER BURNSIDE   Goodbye, Yankee-Girl!
>   (*The watchers follow the hunt with fearful fascination as they sing a round*)

JEFF (*Singing*)
> Look at her go,
> Look at her fly,
> Out of the woods,
> Into the sky;
> Look how she's bobbin' her head,
> Flappin' her feet,
> She must be glued
> To the seat!

PATRICK
> Fall off, Auntie Mame,
> Fall off,
> Fall off,
> Fall off,
> Fall off, Auntie Mame,
> Fall off,
> Before you break your neck!

FAN
> She's ruined your bougainvillaea
> And she's smashed your plums—

MOTHER BURNSIDE
> Hell!

FAN
> She's tramplin' your petunias
> And she's mashed your mums—

MOTHER BURNSIDE
> Damn!

But I'm gonna laugh the loudest
When the judgment comes

MOTHER BURNSIDE and FAN
For that yella-bellied Yankee gal—

GIRLS
Giddyap, Lightnin' Rod!
They went west,
You go east,
Do your stuff, Lightnin' Rod,
And giddyap,
Giddyap,
You little, dear little, crazy beast.

FAN (*Speaking*) She's passing everybody.

MOTHER BURNSIDE She's passing the Master of the Hounds.

JEFF Mighty bad form, passing the Master.

PATRICK She's passing the dogs!

MOTHER BURNSIDE (*Astounded*) Mother of Jefferson Davis, she's passing the FOX!

(*They sing one chorus together, topped by:* FALL OFF! *The music screams to a peak, then cuts. All are stunned and impressed*)

PATRICK Auntie Mame! Auntie Mame!

MAME

MOTHER BURNSIDE (*Converted*) Astounding. First time in the history of the South anyone's brought back the fox—*alive!*

(BEAU *comes on, followed by* HUNTSMEN *carrying the ruffled but happy* MAME, *who carries the tiny fox in her arms*)

BEAU (*Proudly*) Didn't I tell you she's a marvel?

PATRICK (*Patting the fox*) How'd you do it, Auntie Mame? How'd you catch him?

MAME Well, darling, all those big horses and dogs were chasing after this little fella. And there he was, all of a sudden, and I looked down at him and he looked up at me, and we sort of struck up a friendship.

MOTHER BURNSIDE Fetch me my shawl, somebody, I feel the wind of change.

BEAU Family! Friends! This lovely lady has restored elegance and humanity to the gentlemanly sport of the hunt. (*Some cheers*) Mame Dennis. I should like to ask you—well, to become the wife of Beauregard Jackson —uh—uh . . .

ALL (*Helpfully*) Pickett.

BEAU Oh, yes, Pickett—thank you, family—BURNSIDE.

MAME (*Fast*) Yes!!!

MAME

(SALLY CATO *is furious; she throws aside her riding crop and stalks off*)

BEAU   Ah'll make you happy, Mame dear. For a honeymoon, we'll take a year, maybe two, and go clear around the world. Just you and me.

MAME   That's wonderful, Beau.
(*All congratulate the happy pair. Only* PATRICK *is left alone, and he wanders to the side of the stage*)

BEAU (*Projecting jubilantly*)   Listen, everybody! On this plantation, in this county, in this whole blamed state, today's date on the little old calendar is hereby declared officially as—MAME DAY!
(*The music begins*)

MAME (*Impressed*)   Mame Day! Isn't that wonderful, Patrick?

PATRICK (*Bravely*)   Wonderful, Auntie Mame.

BEAU (*Expansively*)   You know why, Mame? Because you've done more for the South than anyone since Robert E. Lee!

BEAU and ALL (*Singing*)
You coax the blues right out 'a the horn,
Mame,
You charm the husk right off 'a the corn,
Mame,
You've got the banjos strummin'

72

MAME

And plunkin' out a tune to beat the band,
The whole plantation's hummin'
Since you brought Dixie back to Dixie Land;

You make the cotton easy to pick,
Mame,
You give my old mint julep a kick,
Mame,
Who ever thought a Yankee
Would put our little Dixie belles to shame?
You've made us feel alive again,
You've given us the drive again,
To make the South revive again,
Mame!

> (BEAU *offers* MAME *his arm and they stroll elegantly as* BEAU *sings*)

BEAU

You brought the cakewalk back into style,

ALL

Mame!

BEAU

You make the weeping willow tree smile,

ALL

Mame!

BEAU

Your skin is Dixie satin,
There's rebel in your manner and your speech,
You may be from Manhattan, but
Georgia never had a sweeter peach;

73

MAME

ALL

You make the old magnolia tree bud,
Mame,
You make camelias bloom in the mud,
Mame,
You make the bougainvillaea
Turn purple at the mention of your name . . .

GIRLS

We're bakin' pecan pies again,
Tonight the chicken fries again,

MOTHER BURNSIDE (*Brandishing her cane*)
This time the South will rise again—

ALL

Mame!

BOYS (*Patter style*)
Well, shut my mouth
And freeze my face
You've brought some elegance to the place
There's sowbelly, hominy, catfish and tripe,
Mame!
Well, shut my mouth
And damn my eyes
You've made the price of tobacco rise
The old watermelon is suddenly ripe,
Mame!
And down on the levee
A beautiful bevy

74

Of crinolined ladies has flocked
The way that they're squealin'
They give me the feelin'
The Robert E. Lee must've docked
The strummin' and ringin'
The hummin' and singin'
Is startin' to get out 'a hand

ALL

Since you brought Dixie back to Dixie Land . . .

You make our black-eyed peas and our grits,
Mame,
Seem like the bill of fare at the Ritz,
Mame,
You came, you saw, you conquered,
And absolutely nothing is the same;
Your special fascination 'll
Prove to be inspirational,
We think you're just sensational,
Mame!

> (BEAU *and* ALL *sweep into a jubilant celebration,
> banjos strumming and all stops out. The languid
> manner of the plantation people has turned into the
> electricity of a cakewalk. Even* MOTHER BURNSIDE
> *throws away her cane and does an exuberant kick
> or two*)

BEAU and ALL

You coax the blues right out 'a the horn,
Mame,

You charm the husk right off 'a the corn,
Mame,
You've got the banjos strummin'
And plunkin' out a tune to beat the band,
The whole plantation's hummin'
Since you brought Dixie back to Dixie Land;

You make the cotton easy to pick,
Mame,
You give my old mint julep a kick,
Mame,
Who ever thought a Yankee
Would put our little Dixie belles to shame?
You've made us feel alive again,
And given us the drive again,
To make the South revive again,
Mame,
Mame,
Mame,
Mame,
Mame!

> (MAME *is receiving the adoration, it would seem,
> of the entire South, and her expression shows that
> she hardly believes it's possible. But there they are,
> top hats off and calling to her in tribute. As* BEAU
> *starts to lead her back toward the house,* MAME
> *notices the forlorn* PATRICK *and goes to him*)

PATRICK (*Singing a wistful phrase of "My Best Girl"*)
And if someday
Another beau comes along
Determined to take my place . . .

(*He can't finish. As the music builds,* MAME *puts her arm around* PATRICK, *then reaches out her other arm to* BEAU)

ALL (*Singing*)
We think you're just sensational,
Mame!

Curtain

Act Two

Act Two

The music is continuous from the entr'acte.

PATRICK *sits at a small desk, with a small portable type-writer. He is wearing a small beanie. He types as he sings. The music underscores, with the melody of "Mame."*

PATRICK (*Reading*) To Mrs. Mame Dennis Burnside, care of American Express, Cairo. Dear Auntie Mame. (*Singing*)

> In English Lit I'm in the top ten—
> I got a B-plus average again—
> Tahiti sounds the greatest
> Of all the crazy places that you've been,
> Wait til you hear the latest . . .
> I think I've got a whisker on my chin!
>> (*Like figures in a Swiss clock, the small boy, small desk and small typewriter rotate out of sight, to be replaced by a larger desk, a larger typewriter and a considerably larger* PATRICK, *wearing a larger beanie. He is now a handsome nineteen*)

PATRICK To Mrs. Mame Dennis Burnside, Raffles Hotel, Singapore. Dear Auntie Mame. (*Singing*)

> I find it's getting harder to cram—
> I flunked my Latin grammar exam—
> My glands are in a hurry,
> My voice has sort of taken on a roar,
> The girls I date, don't worry,

Are socially decidedly top drawer.

And by the way, you'll never guess who my roommate is here at Rumson U.!
> *(The gangling* JUNIOR BABCOCK *ambles into* PATRICK's *room carrying three exotic-looking letters for* PATRICK *and one grubby-looking postcard for himself)*

JUNIOR Ya hit the jackpot, Dennis. Three more letters from your Aunt.

PATRICK *(Taking the letters, scanning the postmarks)* Pago Pago. Shanghai. Singapore.

JUNIOR Save me the stamps, will ya?

PATRICK *(Opening one of the letters)* What ever happened to your cigar-band collection, Babcock?

JUNIOR I gave it up when I started smoking.
> *(*JUNIOR *goes off.* PATRICK *starts reading a letter. The lights come up on the opposite side of the stage.* MAME *and* BEAU *seem to be on a street in Singapore.* BEAU *is snapping pictures;* MAME, *in bizarre traveling clothes, is avidly reading a letter)*

MAME Do you know who Patrick's rooming with at college, Beau? That little son-of-a-banker Babcock. We've got to be getting home.

BEAU But Mame honey, we've almost broken the world's

82

long-distance honeymoon record. And I'm just dyin' to get a crack at that little ol' Matterhorn.

MAME   But I feel Patrick needs me. I've got to write him and find out what he wants to be when he grows up.

PATRICK   Auntie Mame, I'm *up.* (*He stands, and he's a towering lad, all right. The lights fade on* MAME *and* BEAU. PATRICK *sings*)
   I'm shaving every morning
   And growing like it's going out of style;
   The debs all seem to go for me,
   Give France a big hello for me,
   A hug to Uncle Beau for me . . .

Your loving nephew, Patrick. (*A sober* MR. BABCOCK *comes in.* PATRICK *turns to see him, surprised*) Mr. Babcock!
      (JUNIOR *enters, quickly hiding a cigarette behind his back*)

JUNIOR   Hi, Pop. What're you doin' here?

BABCOCK   Leave us alone, will you, Junior? There's something I've got to tell Dennis here.

JUNIOR   Oh, sure.
      (*He backs out of the room, puzzled.* PATRICK *is alone with* BABCOCK)

BABCOCK   I'm afraid I don't have very good news for you, young man.

PATRICK   Auntie Mame! Something's happened to Auntie
Mame.

BABCOCK   She's all right. But that damn fool husband of
hers did a damn fool thing. Fell off a goddam Alp!
(PATRICK *turns away*)

PATRICK (*Softly*)   Uncle Beau—

BABCOCK   Just remember this makes your Aunt a very rich
woman in her own right.
(JUNIOR *appears excitedly, carrying a two-piece
telephone*)

JUNIOR   Hey, Dennis. On the horn. Long distance. (PAT-
RICK, *a little dazed, takes the telephone*) It's the overseas
operator.

PATRICK (*Into the phone*)   Hello? Yes, operator, this is
he! Oh, sure. You bet I want to talk to her! (BABCOCK
takes JUNIOR *offstage*) Auntie Mame? (*He listens*)
You don't have to tell me—I already know. (*He listens
again*) There's just one thing I don't want you to forget,
Auntie Mame—not ever! (*Singing, gently, into the telephone*)
     You're my best girl,
     And nothing you do is wrong,
     I'm proud you belong to me;
     And if a day is rough for me,
     Having you there's enough for me.
          (*A spotlight narrows on his face*)

MAME

And if some day
When everything turns out wrong
You're through with the human race,
Come running to me,
For you'll always be
My best girl.
   (The spotlight goes out)

Scene: The Beekman Place apartment. It is six months later. VERA *and* LINDSAY *wait amid packing boxes and covered furniture.* LINDSAY *is graying nicely.* VERA *has aged about ten minutes. She is in mourning black, including a heavy veil, and is playing the tragedy to the hilt.*

LINDSAY I'm a coward. I should've gone down to the boat to meet her.

VERA Patrick wanted to be alone with her. (*Pointing to a dictaphone and a typewriter*) Lindsay, what is all this?

LINDSAY I got her a dictaphone and a typewriter. Mame's always got to have a project.

VERA How can Mame write a book? She can't even sit still long enough to write a postcard.
(VERA *uncovers a monstrosity of a dragon chair from the Orient and quickly covers it again*)

LINDSAY Well, she's going to have help.

VERA What Mame needs is a friend, a bosom friend. And I'm going to be *better* than a friend—a *sister!*
(*The doorbell chimes.* LINDSAY *goes to answer it*)

86

LINDSAY   She won't recognize you.
> (VERA *strikes a tragic pose and throws open her arms*)

VERA   Mame, you poor tragic darling. *Sister* is here! (AGNES GOOCH *schlumps in, wearing a shapeless overcoat and clutching a shorthand pad*) My God, she can't have changed that much.

AGNES   I've been going to Speed-o.

LINDSAY   I sent her to this secretarial school, so she could master shorthand. Agnes, do you think you can take down every word Mrs. Burnside says?

AGNES   Oh, Speed-o won't let anybody out who can't do at least a hundred words a minute. (*To* VERA) I'm over two hundred.

VERA   You're not!
> (AGNES *takes off her coat and flips open her shorthand pad, ready to begin*)

PATRICK   (*From offstage*) Welcome home, Auntie Mame.

MAME   (*From offstage*) Beekman Place! Dear, loyal Beekman Place.

VERA   Everybody smile.

MAME   (*From offstage*) Just sitting here, waiting for me.

87

MAME

VERA Nobody cry! (MAME *sweeps in, all in white. The ivy-league* PATRICK *follows.* ITO *follows with the luggage.* VERA *bursts into sobs*) Mame darling. You look awful!

MAME Vera, my old, old, *old* friend. And Lindsay, how distinguished you look.

LINDSAY Welcome home.

MAME And Agnes! (AGNES *dutifully mouths and scribbles "And Agnes."* MAME *notices the dictaphone and typewriter*) What's all that?

LINDSAY These are the tools of your new trade. You're going to write a book, Mame, and I'm going to publish it. Your memoirs.

PATRICK Nobody's had a more exciting life than you, Auntie Mame. I think it'd be terrific.

VERA And think of all the fascinating people you've known. Like me.

LINDSAY And it would take your mind off yourself.

MAME (*Suspiciously*) Oh, I see—this is some kind of trumped-up occupational therapy.

LINDSAY No, no . . .

MAME Like hooking rugs. (*Dismissing the idea*) My memoirs. (*Suddenly changing her mind and getting up*)

Angela Lansbury, Jerry Lanning, Johanna Douglas,
and John C. Becher, as MAME, PATRICK, MRS. UPSON,
and MR. UPSON.

What a marvelous idea. I'll dedicate my book to Beau and all the glorious times we had together.

LINDSAY   Writing isn't easy, Mame—it takes months of grueling concentration.

MAME   (*Her eyes lighting up*)   Let me see, let me see. (AGNES *follows her, scribbling furiously every word* MAME *says*) Chapter One, Page One. (AGNES *writes*) Well, I'll be damned, Lindsay. This isn't so difficult after all. (*Wheeling on* AGNES) What are you writing, Agnes?

AGNES   (*Reading her shorthand by rote*)   "Chapter One, Page One, well, I'll be damned, Lindsay, this isn't so difficult after all, what are you writing, Agnes?"

VERA   She *is* fast.

PATRICK   Auntie Mame, you're off and running.

MAME   Oh, Patrick, do you really think I should? You heard Lindsay. It'll take up all my time, and I really came home just to be with you.

PATRICK   You can't exactly *be* with me. No women allowed in the dorm.

MAME   You're all grown up. You don't need me any more. (AGNES *is at* MAME's *elbow, taking down every word in frantic shorthand*) Agnes, how do we turn you off?

89

LINDSAY I'm going right over and announce your book to
my publishing house.
(LINDSAY *exits*)

PATRICK Goodbye for now, Charlotte Brontë.
(PATRICK *goes off*)

MAME (*Dreaming*) Literature! Literature! You know,
Vera, I may even let myself go prematurely gray.
(MAME *takes off her furs and gloves*)

VERA (*Tragically*) Mame. Mame do you forgive me?

MAME For *what*, darling?

VERA Oh, I've had regrets. I tell you I've lost many a
beauty sleep, tossing and turning, because I was so cruel
to you—that terrible time in New Haven.

MAME Vera dear, you've lost beauty sleep? It hardly
shows.

VERA Well, the point is—we forgive each other, Mame.
Let's have a drink to celebrate our reconciliation.

MAME Oh, I've sworn off.

VERA Good idea.

MAME It's such a good idea, let's drink to it. (*They cross
to the bar.* VERA *pours two huge glasses full*) Agnes, do
you care for a drink?

90

AGNES   Oh, thank you no. I think I'll just go fix myself a Dr. Pepper.
> *(She backs out of the room, fascinated by these two women of the world.* MAME *and* VERA *clink glasses)*

VERA   It's like old times.

MAME   Friendship like ours is very rare.
> *(They drink, and start getting pleasantly tipsy)*

VERA   What's the female equivalent to Damon and Pythias?

MAME   Daphnis and Chloe?

VERA   I think one of 'em was a fella.

MAME   The wonderful thing is that you and I, Vera, can say *anything* to each other.

VERA   Absolutely *anything*. Just be careful what you say.

MAME and VERA *(Both sing)*
> We'll always be bosom buddies,
> Friends, sisters and pals,
> We'll always be bosom buddies,
> If life should reject you,
> There's me to protect you—

VERA
> If I say that your tongue is vicious,

MAME
>
> If I call you uncouth,

MAME and VERA
>
> It's simply that
> Who else but a bosom buddy
> Will sit down and tell you the truth!

VERA
>
> Tho' now and again I'm aware that my candid opinion
>   may sting,

MAME
>
> Tho' often my frank observation might scald,
> I've been meaning to tell you for years . . . you
>   should keep your hair natural like mine—

VERA
>
> If I kept my hair natural like yours . . . I'd be bald!
> But darling,

MAME and VERA
>
> We'll always be dear companions,
> My crony, my mate,
> We'll always be harmonizing,
> Orphan Annie and Sandy,
> Like Amos 'n Andy—

VERA
>
> If I say that your sense of style's
> As far off as your youth,
> It's only that

MAME

Who else but a bosom buddy
Will tell you the whole stinkin' truth!

MAME

Each time that a critic has written, "Your voice is
the voice of a frog!"
Straight to your side to defend you I rush,
You know that I'm there every time that the world
makes an unkind remark:
When they say Vera Charles is the world's greatest
lush,
It hurts me.

VERA

And if I say your fangs are showing,
Mame, pull in your claws,
It's simply that
Who else but a bosom buddy
Would notice the obvious flaws!

MAME

I feel it's my duty to tell you, it's time to adjust
to your age,
You try to be Peg O' My Heart when you're Lady
Macbeth,
Exactly how old are you, Vera? The truth.

VERA

Well, how old do you think?

MAME

I'd say somewhere in-between forty and death!

93

VERA

>But sweetie,
>I'll always be Alice Toklas
>If you'll be Gertrude Stein,
>And tho' I'll admit I've dished you,
>I've gossiped and gloated,
>But I'm so devoted!

MAME

>And if I say that sex and guts
>Made you into a star,
>Remember that
>Who else but a bosom buddy
>Will tell you how rotten you are!

MAME and VERA

>Just turn to your bosom buddy
>For aid and affection,
>For help and direction,
>For loyalty, love,
>And forsooth,
>Remember that
>Who else but a bosom buddy
>Will sit down and level,
>And give you the devil,
>Will sit down and tell you the truth!
>>(*At the climax of the song,* MAME *and* VERA *collapse onto the couch.* AGNES *returns from the kitchen with a bottle of Dr. Pepper*)

MAME   Vera, it's amazing. When I think of all the same men we dated, and still remained so inseparable.

VERA Mame! I *never* dated the same man you did.

MAME How about Carlo, that sexy Argentinian with all those shoulders?

VERA (*Indignant*) Carlo! I never dated Carlo. I *married* him, I never dated him.
(AGNES, *fascinated by the conversation, giggles. They both turn and look at her*)

AGNES Oh, excuse me. But listening to you ladies makes me all goose-pimply. Y'see, I never had one.

VERA Never had one *what*?

AGNES A date. With a member of the opposite—you-know-what. (MAME *and* VERA *look at each other; then each takes another long drink, simultaneously. Then they get an inspiration and get up.* AGNES *is baffled as the two women circle her*) Mrs. Burnside, is anything wrong?

MAME Agnes, you're coming out!

AGNES (*Clutching the side of her dress*) Where?

VERA (*Taking off* AGNES' *glasses*) Why, Gooch, you have lovely eyes. Take those glasses off and leave them off forever.

AGNES But, Miss Charles, I can't see anything out of my right eye.

VERA   Who can? Look out of your left one!

MAME   (*Pointing to* AGNES' *shoes*) What do you call *those* things?

AGNES   Orthopedic oxfords.

MAME   Kick 'em off. (*Baffled,* AGNES *complies.* MAME *pulls her dress tight*) My goodness, Agnes—you *do* have a bust. Where have you been hiding it all these years? (AGNES *breaks away, cowering behind the couch*) All your clothes off, Agnes.

AGNES   Mrs. Burnside! There's a man in the house.

MAME   Don't be a goose, Agnes. Get these clothes off and keep them off. (MAME *and* VERA *peel off* AGNES' *clothes; she stands trembling in a shapeless slip.* MAME *calls*) Ito! Come in here. We've got some work to do.
   (ITO *scurries in from the kitchen*)

AGNES   I don't have a very clear picture of what's going on.

VERA   When we're through with you, honey, men will be breaking down your door.

AGNES   What about my virtue?

MAME   Virtue! There's nothing wrong with a harmless smooch.

AGNES   Oh, just the idea of it makes me so nervous, I could die.

MAME Have a date first—then die. (MAME *hands her a drink*) This'll calm you down.

AGNES But spirits do the most terrible things to me. I'm not the same girl.

MAME What's wrong with that?

AGNES (*Turning to* VERA, *the bibing expert*) Will it mix with Dr. Pepper?

VERA (*Emphatically*) He'll love it.
      (AGNES *drinks it down in one gulp.* MAME *pummels her face*)

MAME We really should do something about her complexion. For God's sake, Agnes, close your pores. Ito, go upstairs. Drag out that sexy gown I sent from Paris. And get all my cosmetics: face creams, eyebrow pencils, lipstick.

VERA And a chisel.
      (ITO, *giggling, races up the stairs*)

MAME (*Striking a pose*) Tonight, Agnes, you can be the Queen of Rumania!
      (AGNES *tries to imitate the regal pose but immediately gives up, a coward to the core*)

AGNES Mrs. Burnside, I think I know what you're suggesting I do—and I just don't think I can do anything so —suggestive.

97

MAME   Agnes, where's your *spine?* Here you've been living in the same house with me all these years, and you don't understand what I believe in. LIVE! That's what I believe.

AGNES   Live?

MAME   Yes! Life is a banquet, and most poor sons-of-bitches are *starving* to death! Live!
(ITO, *at the head of the stairs, giggles, waving a pair of silk stockings like two banners*)

AGNES   Live?

VERA   Live!

MAME, AGNES and VERA   LIVE!
(AGNES *races up the stairs, intoxicated by the idea*)

MAME   We're the greatest team since Romulus and Remus.

VERA   I'm *sure* one of *them* was a fella! (*Singing*)
I've patiently watched you for years with those asinine projects of yours,
From orphans to health food you've searched for a niche,

MAME
I feel that my search will be over the moment I've finished my book,

98

I'll write about us . . . and of who is the bitchier
bitch!

VERA (*After thinking about it*) I concede.
(MAME *is unsure whether this is a compliment or
an insult; she thinks about it as they dance*)

MAME and VERA
If life should reject you,
There's me to protect you—
(*The dance continues. Suddenly* AGNES *appears at
the head of the stairs in a sexy red dress. They stop,
amazed. The music slinks into a bump and grind
version of "Bosom Buddies" as* AGNES *moves her hips
and joins* MAME *and* VERA *for the finale of the
dance: a trio in red, white and black. They strut off
in the best burlesque-esque style. It's as if* AGNES
has joined the team. The lights fade)

Scene: MAME's *apartment, six months later. It has been transformed into a literary shrine.*

The ELEVATOR BOY *comes onstage carrying a small table, followed by* ITO *lugging a huge bust of Voltaire.* ITO *goes to the desk and picks up a manuscript the size of the Manhattan phone book. Hearing somebody coming, he puts it down and pretends to be arranging flowers.*

MAME *enters, looking like Elizabeth Barrett Browning.*

MAME   Oh, Ito. I hope the human race is ready for my book.

ITO *(As he exits)*   Oh yes, Missy. Highly educational.
    (MAME *goes to the typewriter and gets to work.*
    VERA *staggers down the stairs, morning-after, as
    usual)*

VERA *(Foggily)*   What time is it? What *day* is it?

MAME   Vera, I'm working.

VERA   On what?

MAME *(Proudly)*   Chapter Two.

VERA *(Incredulously)*   Chapter Two! It took you six months to write Chapter One!

MAME   Flaubert spent thirteen years on *Madame Bovary!*

VERA   How did she stand it? (MAME *clicks away merrily at the typewriter.* VERA *sinks to the couch*) Every time I read a book, I always skip that "I was born" jazz and turn immediately to the sexy part. You know—when the girl is twelve.
(*The doorbell chimes.* ITO *scurries to answer.* LINDSAY *comes in, in a summer suit, carrying an attaché case*)

LINDSAY   Good afternoon, ladies. I dropped by to see how my favorite authoress is doing.

MAME   Oh, swimmingly, Lindsay.
(*She types the end of a sentence as she kisses* LINDSAY)

LINDSAY   Great. But why are you typing yourself?

MAME   Well, after Agnes left I just couldn't face a new secretary. All this material is so intimate.

LINDSAY   Exactly what happened to Agnes?

MAME   Well, we're not sure. We kinda re-designed her, launched her, and except for one postcard we haven't heard from her for six months. (*Taking a picture postal from a drawer*) It says: "I'm trying to do everything you taught me." (*Flipping the card*) It's from the Shangri-La Motel in East Stroudsburg, Pennsylvania.
(PATRICK *comes in, bubbling with excitement*)

PATRICK   Hi, everybody.

MAME   Hello, darling.

PATRICK   Auntie Mame, Uncle Lindsay, Auntie Vera. Hope you're not too busy—'cause I've got some terribly important news.
>   (MAME *gets up eagerly and goes to him*)

VERA   I hope it's gossip.

PATRICK   It is. About me. I've got a girl.

MAME   I suspected it.

PATRICK   It's not just *a* girl, it's *the* girl. Her name is Gloria Upson. And you're going to meet her today.

MAME   I hope you didn't leave her sitting in the car.

PATRICK   I dropped her off at her girl friend's on Park Avenue. She wanted to get spruced up before she met you.

MAME   (*Heading toward the stairs*)   Well, I'd better do some sprucing up on my own.
>   (*The doorbell chimes.* ITO *goes to answer it*)

PATRICK   (*Starting toward the door*)   I'll bring Gloria back in about ten or fifteen minutes, okay?

MAME   I'll have my face all organized.
(AGNES *waddles into the room carrying a suitcase.
She is sheepish, tentative, and about six months
pregnant. All freeze*)

VERA   Omigod, it's the Queen of Rumania!

MAME   Agnes, dear, what happened?

AGNES (*Plaintively*)   I opened a new window. (*Turning
to* MAME) I wanted you to be the first to know.
(MAME *gestures with her head and the men tact-
fully leave the room*)

MAME   Now, Agnes, everything's going to be all right.

AGNES (*Looking back toward the men*)   Do you think
they all noticed?

MAME   Don't worry, Agnes. (*She takes* AGNES' *arm, leading her to the sofa*) Sit right down here and tell me
exactly what happened.

AGNES   I'll try. (*Singing*)
With my wings resolutely spread, Mrs. Burnside,
And my old inhibitions shed, Mrs. Burnside,
I did each little thing you said, Mrs. Burnside,
I lived! I lived! I lived!

I altered the drape of
A drop of my bodice,
And softened the shape of my brow;
I followed directions

And made some connections,
But what do I do now?

Who'd think this Miss Prim would
Have opened a window
As far as her whim would allow?
And who would suppose it
Was so hard to close it?
Oh, what do I do now?

I polished and powdered and puffed myself—
If life is a banquet, I stuffed myself!

I had my misgivings,
But went on a field trip
To find out what living's about;
My thanks for the training,
Now, I'm not complaining,
But you left something out . . .
Instead of wand'ring on with my lone remorse
I have come back home to complete the course!
Oh, what do I do . . .

Mrs. Burnside,
I traveled to hell in my new veneer,
And look what I got as a souvenir!

But still I'll defend you
As guide and instructor,
Would I recommend you . . . and how!
Although I was leery,
I thrived on your theory

That life can be a wow:
You said "There's nothing wrong with a harmless
    smooch,"
So I'm gonna call him "Burnside Gooch,"
But what do I do now?

(LINDSAY, PATRICK *and* ITO *re-enter.* MAME *and*
VERA *join them for a whispered family conference*)

LINDSAY (*Discreetly*) Patrick and I have been discussing
this, and I'll make some arrangements for a place for
Agnes to stay.

VERA I know a darling Jesuit priest who runs a fascinating
home for fallen women.

MAME I do not consider Agnes *fallen.* On the contrary.

PATRICK Auntie Mame, don't tell me Agnes is going to
live here?

MAME I'll insist on it. Where else would she go in her
friendless condition? Ito, help our little mother up the
stairs.
    (ITO *and* AGNES *start up the stairs, cautiously*)

AGNES You're befriending me.

MAME Hell, yes. Why should the Jesuits have all the fun?
What a lovely, lovely feeling. After all these years to
have a nursery again.
    (ITO *and* AGNES *disappear at the top of the stairs*)

LINDSAY (*Closing his eyes*) What a project!

MAME   I hope you all approve of what I'm doing. Because, after all, it's entirely my fault.

VERA   Really, Mame!

MAME   *I* planted the seed of adventure in that girl's soul. I know it's biologically impossible, but ethically, I'm the father of her child.

PATRICK (*Uncomfortably, starting out*)   I guess I'll be buzzing along.

MAME   Patrick dear, I'll be waiting to meet Gloria.

PATRICK (*Evasively*)   Well, with the excitement and everything, it's a little late now. Let's make it another time.

MAME   Oh? What evening would you like to bring your girl by?

PATRICK   I'm not exactly sure, Auntie Mame. Uh—this is Gloria's busy week.

MAME   Thursday would be perfect for me.

PATRICK (*Too hastily*)   Oh, no. Gloria works as a nurse's aide every third Thursday.

MAME   Isn't that nice. Friday then.

PATRICK   On Friday she rests up from Thursday. Tell you what I'll do, Auntie Mame. They're very social. They give lots of parties.

MAME   Who do?

PATRICK   The Upsons. Gloria's folks. I'll get you invited to their place up in Connecticut. So you can meet 'em all properly. Okay?
(*He kisses* MAME's *cheek*)

MAME (*Softly*)   "Properly"?

PATRICK (*Starting out*)   I'll call you.

LINDSAY   I'll ride down with you. (*To* MAME, *as he leaves*) Goodbye, Little Father.

MAME   Vera, what am I going to do?

VERA   You've got to do things "properly." You'll have to invade Connecticut!
(*The lights fade*)

SCENE 4

Scene: The Upson Barn. A gang of Connecticut kids in sports clothes is dancing sedately, Blue Barron style with dips.

At the right, watching benignly, are MR. *and* MRS. UPSON *and* MR. BABCOCK. UPSON *has rolled his bar-cart onstage and is mixing drinks.*

BABCOCK (*To his son*) What do you call that, Junior?

JUNIOR (*Dancing, dipping*) Where ya been, pop? It's the latest dance craze. The Darien Dip!

MRS. UPSON Claude, don't you love to see the kiddies cutting loose?
(*The music finishes to polite applause*)

MR. UPSON (*To* BABCOCK) Why didn't you want us to meet the Aunt, Dwight? She seems like a regular fella—and a looker, too.

MRS. UPSON I hope it's all right to have Gloria's party here in the barn. I don't want Mrs. Burnside to think we live like gypsies.

MR. UPSON You show me a gypsy who lives like we do.

MRS. UPSON Now, Claude Upson, you be genteel in front of Mrs. Burnside.

MR. UPSON Goddam it, I'm always genteel.

BABCOCK Claude, I need a refill.
(UPSON *pours from the shaker into* BABCOCK's *glass*)

MR. UPSON How about you, Doris?

MRS. UPSON I think we chaperones should try to stay sober.

MR. UPSON Say, I meant to ask you, Dwight. Does Mamie drink?

BABCOCK Now and then.
(PATRICK *enters*)

PATRICK My Auntie Mame just loves your place.

MRS. UPSON We're very esteemed to have your Auntie as a chaperone.

PATRICK She's dying to meet Gloria.

MRS. UPSON Oh, what a big day this is for our little Glory. Saying goodbye to her teens and hello to her future aunt-in-law to be.

MAME (*Sweeping on*) My dear Mr. and Mrs. Upson. I can't begin to tell you what I think of your house.

UPSON (*Handing* MAME *a drink*) Mamie, here's your poison. I make my daiquiris with a secret ingredient I learned from this native down in the Virgin Islands—if you'll excuse the expression. I'll tell ya this, there's no sugar in a Claude Upson Daiquiri.

MAME (*Sipping it*) And yet it's so sweet. What ever do you use?

MR. UPSON Guess.

MAME Chocolate ice cream?

MR. UPSON Since we're practically relatives, I'll let you in on my little secret. *Honey!*

MAME I beg your pardon?

MR. UPSON That's my secret. Strained honey. Course, I use quite a little rum, too!
(GLORIA *enters. She has hair like a Vogue model and seems like Miss Insipid of 1937*)

PATRICK Auntie Mame, this is Gloria.

GLORIA I can't tell you how pleased I am to make your acquaintance.

MAME (*Taking her hand*) I know you're very special to Patrick, and that means you're very special to me, too.

GLORIA Isn't this a *marvy* party that Mums and Daddums are throwing me? And everybody on the guest list is absolutely top-hole.

MAME (*Dazed*) Marvy.

GLORIA Today it's farewell to naïveté and hello to sophistication.

MAME Oh, I can see that.

PATRICK Isn't she beautiful, Auntie Mame?

MAME Oh, yes.

MR. UPSON (*Nudging* BABCOCK) Wait'll we tell Mamie the surprise!

MRS. UPSON Not yet, Claude, not yet.

MAME And what lovely hair.

GLORIA Do you like it? The secret is the shampoo. You'll never guess what I use.

MAME Strained honey?

GLORIA Beer! I just pour it and pour it and pour it, and the beer just foams and foams and foams. Daddums says it looks like the bubbles are coming right out of my brain.
    (UPSON *laughs uproariously and pantomimes the glorious picture*)

MRS. UPSON (*Passing an hors d'oeuvres tray*) I made these especially for you, Mamie.

MAME

MAME My, my—don't they look delicious. What *are* they?

MRS. UPSON Well, I take two cans of tuna fish and put them through the meat grinder, then add clam juice and peanut butter.
    (MAME *drops hers into the pocket of* PATRICK's *cardigan sweater as he feeds* GLORIA *an hors d'oeuvre*)

MR. UPSON (*Lifting his glass*) Mamie, I want to make a toast. To the good life. For us and ours.

BABCOCK And we damn well better protect it.

MR. UPSON Did you bring all the legal stuff, Dwight?

BABCOCK It's in my briefcase. (*To the* UPSONS) Needs both your signatures.

MRS. UPSON My, my, I feel so important. Oh, Mamie, would you excuse us for a minute, please?

MAME Oh, of course.

MR. UPSON Think you can chaperone all by yourself?

MAME I'll do my best.

MR. UPSON Fine, fine. We'll be back in a jiffy with a little surprise.
    (BABCOCK *and the* UPSONS *go off. The music starts*)

112

JUNIOR (*To* MAME) I'll bet you didn't recognize me. I'm Patrick's roommate.

MAME Junior Babcock! What are you collecting these days?

JUNIOR Women of the world. Care to dance?

MAME Why, thank you. (*They dance, sedately, at arm's length*) Why are we dancing this way?

JUNIOR Well, it's the way my folks do it, and the Upsons —and well, the older generation.

MAME Didn't you notice? The older generation just left.

DANCER Stop hogging her, Babcock!
(*The* DANCER *grabs* MAME *and starts to jitterbug with her*)

JUNIOR Hey, that's Patrick's Aunt!

PATRICK (*Alarmed*) Auntie Mame!

JUNIOR Handle with care! Show a little respect for age!

MAME Age? What age? (*Singing*)
I have the feeling that time has halted,
I'd like two straws and a chocolate malted,
'Cause that's how young I feel.
I feel like peckin' and bunny huggin',

And lindy hoppin' and jitterbuggin',
'Cause that's how young I feel.
I'm mad for that big band beat,
Wanna ride in a rumble seat—
(Sheldon's got the Chevvy)
Love a face full of frozen custard,
To have a hot dog with sand and mustard,
And ride the Ferris wheel,
Oh honey, 'cause that's how young I feel!

MAME and ALL
I'm ready to ask my mom
Can I go to the junior prom—
(Sheldon's got the Chevvy)
Love a coonskin to knock about with,
To start each morning by giving out with
A Rudy Vallee squeal
(Ahhhhhhh)
Oh honey, 'cause that's how young I feel!
(*The* KIDS, *admiring their free-living chaperone,
cut up the stage with her. But* PATRICK *takes*
GLORIA *away. The dance climaxes with* MAME
proving she's younger than any of them)

KIDS Wow, what a chaperone! Boy, she's really young!
That's the kind of chaperone to have!
(*The* UPSONS *and* BABCOCK *re-enter with some
legal-looking papers*)

MR. UPSON (*Projecting*) Kiddies! The picnic tables are all
set up on the far lawn. Last one to get his hot dog doesn't
get any mustard!

(The KIDS *race off except for* GLORIA *and* PATRICK, *who are smooching)*

MRS. UPSON Mamie dear, do you think we chaperones oughta stop the kiddies from acting so lovey-dovey?

MR. UPSON Good for 'em. Warm 'em up for the wedding.

MAME *(Pale)* Wedding?

MRS. UPSON Claude! You went and said it. You spilled the surprise.

BABCOCK *(Nervous)* Well, she's gonna know sooner or later.

MAME *(To* BABCOCK) It's nice of you to keep me informed.

MRS. UPSON *(Sitting)* And Mamie dear, I've planned the most beautiful wedding. I'm already starting to cry.

MAME *(Also sitting)* So am I.

MRS. UPSON Your Patrick and our little Glory will be joined at the Church the Heavenly Rest in East Mountebank. You'll love it, Mamie.
 *(*GLORIA *and* PATRICK *approach their elders)*

GLORIA It's the most restricted community in our part of Connecticut.

MAME I'll get a blood test.

MR. UPSON But we haven't left you out of our plans, Mamie.

BABCOCK Claude and I have the wedding present all figured out.

MR. UPSON (*Sitting*) We're gonna get together, you and me, Mamie—and buy the kiddies—*that!*

MAME What?

MR. UPSON That valuable lot, right next door. Why, that dandelion patch is one of the choicest pieces of real estate in Mountebank.

MRS. UPSON You see, Mamie, this section is restricted only up to our property line. So we feel we have an obligation to make sure that the wrong people don't—well, *you* know.

MR. UPSON We settle the kiddies in there and at the same time protect the whole neighborhood. Do everybody a favor. We'll buy it together, fifty-fifty, Mamie.

BABCOCK (*Handing a paper to* MAME) Here's the escrow. Claude and Doris have already signed it. Put down your John Hancock—and it's happily ever after.

MAME (*Numbly, taking the paper*) My, my, my. You've

taken care of everything. Do you mind if I discuss this for a minute with Patrick?

MR. UPSON Why sure thing, Mamie. Talk it all out. (*Herding out his wife,* GLORIA *and* BABCOCK) Just give us the high sign when you want another daiquiri.

MRS. UPSON You don't happen to like gin, do you, Mamie?

MAME Love it.

MRS. UPSON After dinner I'll get out the cards and we'll have a little game.
(*She leaves*)

PATRICK (*Awkwardly*) I was going to tell you, Auntie Mame, but—things kept getting in the way.

MAME What things?

PATRICK Well—I knew it would take you a while to get used to the Upsons.

MAME Are *you* used to them? The way they think? The way they live?

PATRICK Auntie Mame, it's very simple. I'm in love. (*His hand goes in his pocket, and comes out smeared with goo*) What the hell is this?

MAME What you're in love with, what you're stuck with—
peanut butter, tuna fish and clam juice, as long as you
live. Is that what you want?

PATRICK Auntie Mame, I've been mixed up with a pretty
crazy bunch of screws and nuts most of my life. I guess
it didn't hurt me—but I damned well want to protect my
little Glory from people like that!

MAME You mean people like *me*.

PATRICK I didn't say that. I'd just rather my Glory didn't
know about a lot of things that ordinary, decent human
beings don't have to know about.

MAME So you want to spend the rest of your life in a
restricted dandelion patch with little Miss Schlitz-head?

PATRICK (*Stunned*) Forget it. Forget you ever met the
Upsons. And forget you ever met *me*.
   (*He strides out*)

MAME (*Calling after him*) Patrick. (*Singing*)
   Where's that boy with the bugle,
   My little love who was always my big romance?
   Where's that boy with the bugle,
   And why did I ever buy him those damn long pants?

   Did he need a stronger hand?
   Did he need a lighter touch?
   Was I soft or was I tough?

Did I give enough?
Did I give too much?

At the moment that he needed me,
Did I ever turn away?
Would I be there when he called
If he walked into my life today?

Were his days a little dull?
Were his nights a little wild?
Did I overstate my plan:
Did I stress the man
And forget the child?

And there must have been a million things
That my heart forgot to say,
Would I think of one or two
If he walked into my life today?

Should I blame the times I pampered him
Or blame the times I bossed him?
What a shame I never really found the boy
Before I lost him . . .

Were the years a little fast?
Was his world a little free?
Was there too much of a crowd,
All too lush and loud,
And not enough of me?

Though I'll ask myself my whole life long
What went wrong along the way,

MAME

Would I make the same mistakes
If he walked into my life today,
If that boy with the bugle
Walked into my life today?
    (*The lights fade*)

SCENE 5

Scene: *The Beekman Place apartment. The room is going through a metamorphosis—to ultramodern. Presiding over this transformation is a trim and unaffected redhead,* PEGEEN RYAN.

AGNES, *a few weeks further along, is sipping a glass of milk.* PEGEEN *pays no attention to her whatsoever, and* AGNES *disappears up the stairs.*

PATRICK *enters, wearing a dinner jacket. He looks around, worried about the changes in décor.*

PATRICK   What the hell's going on?

PEGEEN   Face-lifting. (*Sizing up* PATRICK, *not uncritically*) Oh, you must be the "Little Love."

PATRICK   Are you the new decorator? Did you do all of this?

PEGEEN   (*Grinning*)   For money. (ITO *enters, in livery, carrying a futuristic table*) Right here, Ito—that's fine.

ITO   Oh, missy very happy you here for very important party.
   (ITO *goes off to the kitchen*)

PATRICK (*Scowling at the low sofa*)   What's this supposed to be?

PEGEEN   A sofa. Japanese modern. You find it every place except Japan.

PATRICK (*Panicky*) But the Upsons don't understand modern. They're strictly bitter colonial. Do *you* like it?

PEGEEN   No.

PATRICK You're honest at least, Miss . . . ?

PEGEEN   Pegeen Ryan. Unincorporated.

PATRICK (*Shaking her hand*)   Hi.

PEGEEN   Hi.

PATRICK (*Not letting go of her hand*)   Pegeen Ryan . . . Didn't we meet once?

PEGEEN   Yeah. We both went to Ralph Devine's Laboratory of Life.

PATRICK (*With a slow smile*)   Hey, that's right. I didn't recognize you with all your clothes on. (*He breaks off*) That is, maybe we know each other better'n we thought.

PEGEEN   (*Straight-faced*)   You're—*taller*. Can I have my hand back, if you're through with it?
         (*He lets go*)

PATRICK   Where's my aunt?

PEGEEN   Getting ready for the big blowout.

PATRICK (*Worried*)   Oh, no, this is just going to be a nice, simple little evening at home. (*Calling nervously up the stairs*) Auntie Mame?

PEGEEN   Relax. People get married every day.

PATRICK   I'm not getting married every day. I'm getting married three weeks from Tuesday.

PEGEEN (*Tossing it off as she exits*)   Congratulations.
  (MAME *makes a glittering sweep down the stairs, dressed to the hilt in a smashing hostess gown*)

MAME   Patrick darling! Pipe of peace?

PATRICK   Aw, Auntie Mame—who can stay mad at you? After the fight we had at the Upsons, I felt terrible.

MAME   So did I, dear. But see how nicely things have worked out? And tonight I want everything to be just right for the Upsons.

PATRICK   You're wonderful, Auntie Mame. (*Suddenly worried*) Hey, what about Agnes?

MAME (*Glibly*)   In seclusion, dear. Erase her from your thoughts. (PEGEEN *returns with the ladder and pieces of a mobile*) Patrick, be a little gentleman and help Pegeen, will you?

PATRICK Yeah. Sure. (PATRICK *steadies the ladder as* PEGEEN *climbs to add pieces to the mobile*) That's pretty avant-garde for the Upsons.

AGNES (*Entering at the top of the stairs*) I think it's very unusual.
   (PATRICK *wheels as if he'd been stabbed*)

PATRICK What the hell is Agnes doing here? Auntie Mame, you promised . . .

MAME Agnes, I told you to stay in your room tonight.

AGNES But it's calcium time. And my calcium pills are in the kitchen.

MAME (*Lightly, to* PATRICK) Life's little emergencies.
   (*The doorbell chimes*)

PATRICK My God! They're here!

AGNES (*Helpfully*) I'll get it.

PATRICK Oh, no you don't!
   (PATRICK *leaps to block her*)

AGNES You don't approve of me. I'm not loved.

PATRICK You're loved, Agnes! My God, have you been loved! (*Pleading*) But please, Agnes, cry upstairs!
   (*The wailing* AGNES *has climbed the stairs and goes off. The* UPSONS, GLORIA, *and* MR. BABCOCK—*all in dinner clothes—enter*)

MAME (*With instant poise*) Welcome, welcome to the Burnside Fireside.

MR. UPSON Good to see you, Mamie. You don't look a day older.

MAME Claude, darling. And Doris! How I've been looking forward to this.

PATRICK (*Embracing* GLORIA) Hi, Sweetums.

MAME And little Glory.

GLORIA (*With automated charmlessness*) I can't tell you how pleased I am to see you again.

MAME And our family counsellor through thick and thin. How bully of you to come, Mr. Babcock.

BABCOCK Bully of you to ask me!
     (MAME *waves toward the ladder*)

MAME Won't you all sit down? Oh, I want you to meet Miss Pegeen Ryan. (MRS. UPSON *flops on the low couch and sprawls out flat.* ITO *enters with two trays of hors d'oeuvres, assorted and strange*) Now, Doris, Claude. You were so unbelievably gracious to me in Mountebank, that I had to plan something extra-special for you.
     (*She passes the tray.* GLORIA *takes an hors d'oeuvre*)

GLORIA (*Nibbling one*) Oh, these are scrumptious. Try one of the little striped ones, Mums.

BABCOCK Say, these *are* tasty.

MRS. UPSON Whatever *are* they, Mamie dear?

MAME (*Singing, as she blithely passes them around*)
Pickled python,
Peppered sheep spleen,
Have some owls eggs,
It's today!
I said "Ito, do something exotic,
Just try a little bit harder to please,"
And he's been extra ambitious;
Try these—they're delicious,
    (*All take a bite*)
They're bees!
    (*Some choking and gasping goes on as all stop
    chewing mid-bite. The music has continued. A
    WAITER brings in a tray of tall metal glasses. A
    crowd from* MAME's *first party sweeps into the room
    including:* RALPH DEVINE, *the* BISHOP, *an* ARAB, *a
    couple of* GANGSTERS, M. LINDSAY WOOLSEY *and sev-
    eral show girls*)

ALL (*Singing as they enter*)
And we're livin'!
And we're well, gang,
So raise hell, gang,
While we may—
Call the cops out,
Raise a racket,
Pull the stops out,

VERA (*Sweeping on, singing*)
　It's today!

Mame darling!

MRS. UPSON　Claude. Claude. That's the famous stage star
—what's-her-name!

MAME (*Projecting gaily*)　I won't try to introduce every-
body. But I *do* want you to meet my dearest friend, Vera
Charles. And the celebrated publisher, M. Lindsay
Woolsey.
　　(VERA *poses regally in the center of the stage.*
　　GLORIA *rushes up to her*)

GLORIA　Miss Charles, I've simply *got* to tell you how I
adored you in "Reflected Glory."

VERA (*With a frozen smile*)　Did you, dear?

VERA and MAME　That was Tallulah Bankhead.

MAME　Vera is only a baritone. Can I persuade you to have
a drink, dear?

VERA　Well, maybe just a tiny triple. And anything except
rum. I've just been at the most God-awful party, and all
they had were daiquiris—made with *honey* yet!
　　(ITO *brings* VERA *a giant Scotch.* PEGEEN, *still atop
　　the ladder, is struggling with the mobile*)

MAME　Pegeen, do you need a little help on that ladder?

PEGEEN   No. Just three hands.

MAME   Patrick, lend her one of yours, will you?
    (PATRICK *starts up the ladder, which sways.* PAT-
    RICK *throws his arms around* PEGEEN *to keep her
    from falling*)

GLORIA (*Indignant*)   Well, that's a pretty picture, I *must*
    say!

VERA   Isn't it though? Ladies and gentlemen, I want to
    propose a toast. To this lovely young couple as they start
    up the ladder of life together.

PATRICK (*Hurrying down the ladder*)   No, no, Auntie
    Vera. *This* isn't Gloria. *That's* Gloria.

VERA   Pity. (*She shrugs and lifts her glass*) Well, let's
    have a toast, anyhow. What do you say, Mrs. Upjohn?
    (AGNES *waddles down the stairs. All eyes slowly
    turn to her. The men rise.* PATRICK *is petrified*)

MAME   Now, Agnes, I told you to stay in your room.

AGNES   But you also told me I just *had* to take my calcium
    pills, and they're still in the kitchen.

MAME   Oh, of course.

MR. UPSON (*To* BABCOCK)   Is that a member of the
    family?

BABCOCK Damned if I know.

MR. UPSON It's a member of *somebody's* family.
  (PATRICK *is suffering. But* MAME *tries to make the
  best of it*)

MAME (*Taking* AGNES' *arm*) Everybody, I'd like you to
  meet my secretary. She's a little bit—she's not quite herself at the moment.

MRS. UPSON (*Warmly, to* AGNES) Now, now, we know all
  about these women's things, don't we? (*Sympathetically*) What's your name, dear?

AGNES Gooch.

MRS. UPSON (*Patting the sofa beside her*) You sit right
  over here beside me, Mrs. Gooch. (AGNES *glances down
  at the couch, then slowly lowers herself*) Now tell me,
  what does *Mr.* Gooch do?

AGNES Oh, my father passed on.

MRS. UPSON No, I mean your *husband.*

AGNES (*Wailing*) I'm a *bachelor girl!* And my baby's
  gonna be a little bas . . .
  (MRS. UPSON *gasps. The Puritans look shocked*)

MR. UPSON (*In righteous rage*) Hold it. Hold it. We've
  got some young people here.

BABCOCK (*Hastily*) Claude, as soon as we get him away from the aunt, everything's going to be fine.

PATRICK (*Sweating*) Y'see, my aunt is so big-hearted, whenever anybody's in trouble, she just has to go to the rescue.

MAME *I'm* the one who was rescued. Agnes led me into a whole new project. Do you realize how many girls there are every year who find themselves expecting all by themselves?

VERA Mame, how theatrical of you! All of those fallen angels, finding a haven here in Beekman Place!

PATRICK No, no, no, no.

MAME This is much too big for Beekman Place.

LINDSAY Mame's bought a piece of property up in Mountebank.

MRS. UPSON What? What's that about Mountebank?

MR. UPSON (*To* MAME) You building a place up in our neck of the woods, Mamie?

MAME The Beauregard Burnside Memorial Home for Single Mothers. (*The* UPSONS *stiffen*) How lovely it will be—*hundreds* of girls, romping in that dandelion patch.
(*This does it for the* UPSONS)

MR. UPSON   Are you ready, Doris?

MRS. UPSON   I've been ready for quite a long time.

MR. UPSON (*Heading for the door*)   Come, Glory—we have a long way to go.
   (*The* UPSONS *stride out indignantly*)

BABCOCK (*Exploding*)   For nine years, Mame Dennis Burnside, I've done everything I could to protect this boy from your cockeyed, idiotic nincompoopery! But this is the limit. Now you've ruined everything.

MAME   All you want to do is slam windows in his life. Well, I won't let you do that to my little one. (*Turning toward* PATRICK) No, he's not little any more. And he's not mine. But he's not yours either, Mr. Babcock. And I doubt if he'll let you marry him off to a headful of hair with the I.Q. of a dead flashlight battery!
   (BABCOCK *exits huffily*)

LINDSAY   Did you plan all this, Mame?

MAME   Why would you think that, Lindsay? I always want Patrick to make his own decisions. (*She masks her concern by playing the hostess, passing the tray of hors d'oeuvres*) Python, anyone?
   (*Now she turns to face* PATRICK. *What does he think? She holds her breath*)

PATRICK (*After a pause*)   Thank you, Moon Lady. (*Singing*)

And if someday
Another girl comes along,
It won't take her long to see
That I'll still be found
Just hangin' around
My best girl.
(*During the number, the others have left and*
MAME *and* PATRICK *end up in double spotlights.*
The lights fade)

SCENE 6

Scene: The Beekman Place apartment, 1946. A huge Jackson Pollock-like painting indicates that even the absent MAME *is keeping up with the times.*

PETER *rushes on waving a turban and shouting off to the left.*

PETER   Hey, Mom! Hey, Dad! Look at the wonderful junk Auntie Mame gave me. (*As* PEGEEN *and* PATRICK, *in overcoats, enter,* PETER *puts on the turban*) This is what kids wear for hats in India. Crazy, huh?

PATRICK   Peter, I knew you'd like your Aunt.

PEGEEN (*Correcting him*)   She's your *great*-aunt, Peter.

PETER   She sure is. She's the greatest aunt a guy ever had. Boy, she knows a lot of things I'll bet you don't even know, Dad.

PEGEEN (*To* PATRICK)   Are we going to let her spoil our son the same way she spoiled you?

PATRICK   If she hadn't spoiled me, Pegeen, *I'd* be living in Mountebank and *you'd* be a bachelor girl.
       (MAME *sweeps on in a great traveling coat and fur hat*)

133

MAME Salaam to your Mother, Peter, like Auntie Mame just taught you. (PETER *bows, Indian style, touching his forehead, his chest, and sweeping out his arm*) Ahh, very good, Sahib.

PATRICK Why are you rushing away, Auntie Mame?

MAME *Bell dar-wazay pair carray-ahn,* darling. (*Arm around* PETER) Peter dear, in Hindi that means: "The water oxen are waiting at the gate." Of course, *our* water ox is waiting at La Guardia. TWA Flight 100 for New Delhi.

PEGEEN What do you mean, *our* water ox?

MAME Peter and I just had the most beautiful idea.

PATRICK (*Firmly*) No.

MAME But the boy is *deprived.* He's never even ridden an elephant.

PETER Can I go with Auntie Mame? Can I, Mom? Please? Please? It's just to India!

PEGEEN It's ridiculous! I wouldn't hear of it.

PETER (*Turning to* PATRICK) Dad?

PATRICK You heard your Mother.

PETER (*Wheeling on* PEGEEN) You know what your trouble is, Mom? You don't live, live, *live!* Life is a banquet and most poor sons-of-bitches are *starving* to death.

(PEGEEN *grabs* PETER, *clamping her hands over his mouth.* PATRICK *holds out his hands helplessly: you can't fight Mame-intoxication. Unwillingly,* PEGEEN *lets* PETER *go; he rushes to the arms of* MAME)

PEGEEN   One thing you've got to understand. School begins the day after Labor Day. He's got to be back by then.

MAME   (*Vaguely*) Naturally. Of course. Labor Day. That's sometime in November, isn't it?

PATRICK   Auntie Mame!

MAME   Oh, Peter, what times we're going to have together. And when *your* little boy is ready to take a trip with Auntie Mame, I hope you won't be as antediluvian as your father.

PETER   What's "ante-diluvian," Auntie Mame?

MAME   On the plane, Peter, I'll give you a pad and pencil and you can write down all the words you don't understand.

PATRICK   She hasn't changed! She's the Pied Piper!
(ITO *comes onstage*)

MAME   (*Drawing* PETER *toward the stairs*) I've been shopping all day for your traveling gear. Long pants and —(*Taking a bugle from* ITO)—this.

PETER (*Looking adoringly at the bugle and at* MAME)
Golly!

MAME (*As they climb the stairs slowly*) Oh, my little
love, your Auntie Mame is going to unlock doors for
you. What adventures we're going to have together!
(*Singing*)
> Open a new window,
> Open a new door,
> Travel a new highway
> That's never been tried before . . .
>> (*A glow of light strikes* MAME's *face as she leads*
>> PETER *around a bend in the staircase and upward
>> into new worlds.* PEGEEN *and* PATRICK *wave good-
>> bye as the music swells and the curtain lowers
>> slowly. The music, however, continues. The stair-
>> case rotates out of view, and the curtain rises almost
>> instantly for singing curtain calls, which are an in-
>> tegral part of the play itself. First, the* MARCHERS
>> *parade into view as they did at the beginning of
>> the "Open a New Window" dance.* SINGERS *swirl
>> among* DANCERS, *then come forward to form a line.
>> The melody becomes "It's Today," from "There's a
>> thank you/You can give life." During this, in-
>> dividual bows are taken by the principals. Again
>> the melody changes to "We Need a Little Christ-
>> mas." Then, as the orchestra vamps into "Mame,"
>> the entire line swings into a diagonal line leading
>> upstage toward the right.* MAME *appears in a star-
>> tling new all-white costume, and the entire cast
>> sings "Mame" to her. She kisses her* PATRICKS, *her*

BEAU, VERA, GOOCH *and* ITO, *and grandnephew* PE-
TER: *ah, the zest of* MAME *is perpetual!*

ENTIRE COMPANY   We think you're just sensational,
Mame!
Mame!
Mame!
Mame!

Curtain